Praise for *Being Relational*

"*Being Relational* will forever change the way you think about the person sitting next to or across from you in a mediation or negotiation, as well as how you interact with the people living and working with you. *Warning:* you won't be able to 'un-know' what you will learn in these pages; something inside you is very likely going to shift. Anyone who cares about the quality of her or his work and personal relationships needs to read *Being Relational*—and then let every word soak all the way in."

—**Roxi Bahar Hewertson**, author of *Lead Like It Matters . . . Because It Does* and CEO of Highland Consulting Group, Inc.

"*Being Relational* speaks to the heart of reconciling differences. It moves us from stereotyping to knowing others as they actually are. Bravo to applying the Enneagram map to negotiating interpersonal matters of consequence."

—**Helen Palmer**, teacher of conscious studies and international bestselling author of *The Enneagram: Understanding Yourself and the Others in Your Life* and *The Enneagram in Love and Work: Understanding Your Intimate and Business Relationships*

"*Being Relational* could help just about anyone who deals with other people—or with themselves. It is clear, compelling, and suffused with practical wisdom derived from enormous experience in life and in dealing with conflict."

—**Leonard L. Riskin**, Chesterfield Smith Professor of Law at the University of Florida Levin College of Law and Harris H. Agnew Visiting Professor of Dispute Resolution at Northwestern University School of Law

"Perhaps nowhere in America could we more use a lesson in 'being relational' than Capitol Hill. As partisan squabbling increasingly gets in the way of commonsense solutions, lawmakers could stand to reevaluate their approach to interacting with others with the help of expert mediators Louise Phipps Senft and William Senft. Maybe the 'Seven Ways to Quality Interaction' could even help those of us in office overcome our ideological differences and create 'lasting change' for the American people."

—**C. A. "Dutch" Ruppersberger**, Congressman (MD)

"*Being Relational* is a gem! It distills decades of wisdom into seven simple concepts. By focusing on the skills needed for relationship-building and the personal qualities needed for conflict resolution, the authors have identified essential ingredients for a more peaceful and prosperous planet."

—**David A. Hoffman**, lecturer on law at Harvard Law School and the Program on Negotiation and founder of Boston Law Collaborative, LLC

"In the late 1990s I was a member of a team challenged to deliver a service to a large, important customer. Everyone assumed the customer wanted what we had to offer. A suggestion by a team member allowed us to consider not only what we had to offer, but *how* we might engage and deliver. It was by combining the two that we were successful. *Being Relational* is the first book to bring it all together, giving readers a reasonable path to deliver the *what* and the *how* plus the *why* no matter the circumstances in a simple, clear, and concise manner such that each of us can continue becoming."

—**Margaret Walker**, founder of MLRW Group, member of the board of directors at Methanex Corporation, and former vice president of Engineering Solutions and Technology at The Dow Chemical Company

"In my life and in my practice I have discovered that relationships are among the fundamental necessities that influence our thinking and our behavior. Louise Phipps Senft and William Senft provide tools and techniques that can help us to better understand our interactions with others and what is required to build, enhance, and maintain our relationships. This book guides us toward a path of transformation that leads to a more relational approach to managing and resolving our differences in today's conflict-addicted world."

—**Marvin E. Johnson**, founder of the Center for Alternative Dispute Resolution and former chair of the Advisory Council on Diversity of the Section of Dispute Resolution of the American Bar Association (ABA)

"*Being Relational* brings us back to the basics, but with tremendous nuance, outlining a series of simple, yet profound, principles that will most certainly lead you to greater success. A well thought-out tutorial that centers you on your true self, focusing on caring for others yet with effective intellectual honesty."

—**James A.C. Kennedy**, CEO at T. Rowe Price

"*Being Relational* is a guide for anyone who seeks to convert a lonely individual failure into an inspiring collective success. Human nature will seem less complicated after you read it."

—**Bob Kerrey**, managing director at Allen and Company, co-chair of Issue One Advisory Board, and former U.S. Senator and 35th Governor of Nebraska

"*Being Relational* provides a powerful path to one of life's treasures: *meaningful relationships.* Whether interacting with family, friends, business associates, or adversaries, strong relationships should be part of the outcome and the Senfts eloquently guide us there."

—**Ron Shapiro**, chairman of Shapiro Negotiations Institute and *New York Times* bestselling author

"Conflict and negotiation is inevitable. With the synthesis of so many resources, including their prominent careers, Louise and William have crafted a work of genius, a tool of magnitude and, hopefully, a movement to shift all negotiations into their most optimal outcome. This book is that synthesis, offering a solid system—and more."

—**David M. Corbin**, bestselling author of *Illuminate: Harnessing the Positive Power of Negative Thinking* and *Preventing BrandSlaughter*

"Louise and William Senft have written a book that skillfully details a path forward to repair the broken ways we engage with each other. At the heart of our human suffering is the way we do conflict, whether global societal crisis, economic chaos, polarized political dialogue, racism, extreme religious differences, war, and the breakdown of the family structure. The complexity we experience as a result of the destructive ways that we engage is the key barrier to our planet's well-being. As experienced conflict practitioners and educators, the Senfts' *Being Relational* approach, grounded in theory and science, outlines seven ways that can lead us toward quality dialogue and sustain us through our conflicts to reach the other side."

—**Nan Waller Burnett, M.A.**, mediator, author of *Calm in the Face of the Storm*, and professor at Regis University

"Louise Phipps Senft and William Senft have given us a brilliantly synthesized and hauntingly simple and profound approach for creating greater well-being in every interaction, especially the ones that potentially divide us because of our differences. *Being Relational* is a seminal piece of work on how to make the possibility of quality engagement a reality, even with those you don't like or who are different from you, locally and globally. If you manage people, every person on your team needs to read *Being Relational*; your leadership and interactions will be forever changed for the best."

—**Fernando Hernandez**, director of Supplier Diversity at Microsoft

"Open your minds, your hearts and, dare I say, souls when you read this book. As a scientist, you understand that knowledge and learning is an ever-constant process. Even so, as a human being living and interacting on this earth, certain things are taken for granted; simple things, like how generous, how humble, and how kind you are. The Senfts have heightened my awareness of how much more work I have to do in these areas as well as how high my expectations can and should go. Your relationships, with those you love and with strangers and enemies, the process of your life through interactions with others, is the theme of this book. *Being Relational* challenges us to live at a higher level and to be grounded, clear, and centered within ourselves and to interact from a position of love. Halfway through I experimented with the process in an interaction with my teenage son—a dramatic change in our typical outcome ensued. Start with the 'ORANS—The Image of Being Relational' section at the end, then visualize yourself with that posture as you read. This book could change your life."

—**Mary Ellen P. McNally, Ph.D.**, technical fellow at the Stine Haskell Research Center for the Crop Protection Products business unit at E. I. du Pont de Nemours and Company

"*Being Relational* constantly reminded me of so many missed opportunities over the years to influence lives and outcomes, yet joyfully inspires the reader to embrace the hope and power of building real relationships. Louise and William's delightful book forces us, to paraphrase William F. Buckley, to stand athwart our increasingly disconnected culture and yell, 'stop!' This book will not only change your world, but could change THE world. It is a must-read for anyone who does, or aspires to, lead and influence others."

—**Kelly D. Johnston**, vice president of government affairs at Campbell Soup Company

"*Being Relational* is a seminal contribution not only to the practice of negotiation and dispute resolution but also to our understanding of how we all interact with each other in an increasingly 'hyper-connected' world. Louise Phipps Senft and William Senft bring more than two decades of experience acquired as mediators and problem solvers to their examination of how managers and decision makers need to deal with managing conflict and building relationships. Understanding the distinction the authors make between dealing with people in a transactional fashion and dealing with them in a relational fashion is essential to understanding human relationships in the modern world. The paradox of our era is that providing people with easier access to the Internet and social media only seems to have complicated our interactions with each other. The Senfts' new book provides practical advice on how to cope with the dilemma of handling misunderstandings when the source of those misunderstandings is no longer too little communication but too much. *Being Relational* is required reading for anyone in a leadership role who seeks to build more constructive relationships within organizations, communities, and families."

—**David B. Lipsky**, Anne Evans Estabrook professor of dispute resolution in the School of Industrial and Labor Relations and director of the Scheinman Institute on Conflict Resolution at Cornell University

"Louise Phipps Senft and William Senft take readers to the heart of successful connections within families, communities, and workplaces and provide key skills to create lasting, positive relations. The authors have spent many years empowering people in conflict to find positive change in their lives and guiding others to discover peaceful solutions to the urgent crises now facing our planet."

—**Dr. Joan Goldsmith**, author of *Learning to Lead* and *Resolving Conflicts at Work*

"My experience as a lawyer, mediator, and judge has been that our failure to resolve conflict is not because we are not smart enough or we do not have the means to do so, it is because we do not care deeply enough about our relationship with the other side. In their practical yet profound book *Being Relational*, Louise Phipps Senft and William Senft share with us the qualities necessary to form lasting, meaningful, and productive interactions and thus change. The seven qualities discussed for lasting change are all familiar to us, but seldom are we intentional about calling upon them to change our part of the world. An enjoyable and easy read, you might even find it completing your unspoken thoughts. I would refer to it as *Getting to Yes* for the soul."

—**Michael John Aloi**, circuit court judge in the 16th Judicial Circuit of West Virginia

"Louise and William have written a wise and deeply insightful book. They offer concrete and realistic advice on how all of us can maximize our personal and professional interactions, and create a more collaborative and peaceful world in the process. *Being Relational* is a powerful roadmap on how to bring out the 'better angels' that lie inside all of us."

—**Robert J. Fersh**, president and founder of Convergence Center for Policy Resolution

"As an observer of the increasingly polarized and dysfunctional Congress for almost forty years, I think I can say that the fundamental problem in the institution is the breakdown in quality interaction among the members. Legislators can accomplish far more when they work with each other as individuals rather than operate as political robots relentlessly following their leader or some ideological faction. If members are looking for a guide as to how they might become happier and more productive, they should begin by reading *Being Relational*. Solving the problems faced by our nation and the world requires all of us, in a myriad of ways, to improve our interaction with others, but it is crucial that our leaders learn and utilize these techniques as well."

—**Vic Fazio**, senior advisor at Akin Gump Strauss Hauer and Field LLP and former U.S. Congressman (CA)

"Louise Phipps Senft and William Senft have easily passed author Malcolm Gladwell's '10,000 hour rule' for achieving world-class skill in their field of mediation and conflict resolution. But in this book they use their experience to help us all understand that the techniques they teach to help people address conflicts are the same ones we can use to achieve healthy relationships and harmony in our lives. Thinking of human interactions as relational, rather than as transactional negotiations to gain relative individual success, actually leads to mutual success and happiness. Yes, *Being Relational* is a handbook for living our personal lives. But it is more than that. The techniques it contains apply just as well to the goal of replacing the escalation of conflict with relational responsiveness in politics and in international relations. Its wisdom and approach are that important and valuable."

—**Stuart Butler**, senior fellow at the Brookings Institution, visiting fellow at Convergence Center for Policy Resolution, and former director of the Center for Policy Innovation at the Heritage Foundation

"*Being Relational* is a remarkable work. It is informative, inspiring, and eminently readable. The central theme focuses on the skills and insights one presents in a successful relationship. At one level, the book is a mediator toolbox. Drawing, as it does, on the authors' long experience, and on the rich conflict resolution literature they have mastered, it makes many useful suggestions to sharpen one's practice. On another level, it is a primer on self-awareness and social intelligence. Referencing Jung, Goleman, the Enneagram, and neuroscience, its insights are offered in the narrative, with contemporary illustrations, and the invitation to engage in self-inquiry on thoughtful questions. The book is also a spiritual guide. Drawing this time from timeless wisdom teachings, it deconstructs core values—such as honesty, gratitude, generosity, humility, and kindness—and invites inquiry as to how they apply to us in each of our interactions. This book is a gift to anyone in a relationship, be it marriage, family, business, community, politics, or leadership."

—**William B. Bohling**, commercial mediator and retired judge of the Utah Third District Court

"Transactional versus Relational interaction and the benefits of each is the core theme of this innovational book. Relational interaction clearly comes out on top and provides the basis for successful and strong connections both personally and professionally. *Being Relational* is a masterful resource that provides a guide for us toward increased well-being in all we do."

—**Marsha Firestone, Ph.D.**, founder and president of Women Presidents' Organization and Women Presidents' Educational Organization

"In our fast-paced, digitally connected world, Louise and William remind us of the importance of personal interaction at the human level. Using the tools offered in *Being Relational,* I've seen a marked improvement in my interactions with others both in business and at home, and am introducing the concept to my teams."

—**Dan Taylor**, director of Global Display at Google

"Life is about relationships—to the degree that without love, human beings don't develop properly. In *Being Relational,* husband and wife team Louise Phipps Senft and William Senft study how we interact with one another, offering an exercise in self-discovery. This book will put you on a path to personal, professional, and spiritual development, improving your well-being, all your interactions, and ultimately your relationships."

—**Dr. David Daniels**, clinical professor of psychiatry at Stanford University, leading developer of the Enneagram system of nine personality styles, and author of *The Essential Enneagram*

"Louise and William have offered a thoughtful and loving gift to all of us, in every walk of life, in the framework and principles espoused in *Being Relational,* which can be applied to *all* human interactions. By internalizing and practicing their methods, we can arrive at commonality of understandings among people on opposite sides of ostensibly unbridgeable divides, and are given hope that we can, indeed, further the cause of sustainability for the human race. My deep gratitude to you two!"

—**Riaz Siddiqi**, founder and managing partner of Denham Capital

"*Being Relational* is the cornerstone of investment for anyone wishing to create *paradise* in their home space. Having helped launch the *Chicken Soup for the Soul* series, *Men Are From Mars, The Secret, Outwitting the Devil, Rich Dad Poor Dad,* and other blockbuster titles, I ask all our hundreds of millions of readers to get five copies of *Being Relational* as you will wish to give this gift to those you care for most in your close circles. *Being Relational* is the 'do it now' book of the decade that will keep on giving. Send out 'five to thrive' and everyone will thank you for years and years and years. I so approve of their message."

—**Berny Dohrmann**, chairman of CEO Space International and bestselling author of *Redemption: The Cooperation Revolution*

"Whether it's in politics, business, or simply interacting with our next-door neighbors, we're good at expressing our own views and not so good at hearing—and considering—somebody else's perspective. We have many contacts but few real interactive relationships. The result is division and conflict. This marvelous book identifies clear, effective steps that will make our relationships better and in the process lead to better outcomes for us all individually and collectively. I highly recommend it."

—**Mickey Edwards**, former U.S. Congressman (OK) and vice president of the Aspen Institute

"In David Brooks' *The Road to Character*, Mr. Brooks talks about how our fast-paced, super-segmented lives have increased our focus on résumé virtues to the detriment of eulogy virtues—building our external careers versus our inner character. *Being Relational: The Seven Ways to Quality Interaction & Lasting Change* in many ways completes the circle. Louise and William do a masterful job of showing how, by focusing on seven 'eulogy virtues,' we can significantly improve the meaning and quality of our actions and interactions from the most personal to the most public. So whether you are on an inner journey, looking to improve your relationship with those closest to you or those you interact with in public, this book gives you seven keys that will fit in each and every door."

—**Duf Sundheim**, federal court mediator and political reformer

"In *Being Relational*, Louise Phipps Senft and William Senft reveal important insights on how you can improve relationships in all aspects of your life through the decisions you make on how to interact: by 'Being Engaged, Being Centered, Being Grounded, and Being Clear.' Aspirational and also doable with their thought provoking writing."

—**Sharon Lechter, CPA, CGMA**, CEO of Pay Your Family First, bestselling author of *Think and Grow Rich for Women*, and co-author of *Outwitting the Devil, Three Feet from Gold*, and *Rich Dad Poor Dad*

"It was a joy to read *Being Relational* after using these concepts and techniques for many years to train tribal community mediators and to mediate intra-tribal conflicts in my home community on the Hopi Reservation. *Being Relational* lays out the basic concepts in a clear and easy to follow format and is invaluable information for one's personal growth as well as for honing one's skills as a mediator or even just to be a responsible member of one's community. In a world where we are all expected to compete and become 'winners,' it is a relief to hear a message that, in order for any one of us to truly win, we will need to listen to each other and to care about each other to do it."

—**Patricia Sekaquaptewa**, justice of the Hopi Appellate Court and assistant professor of the Department of Alaska Native Studies & Rural Development at the University of Alaska Fairbanks

"We generally think of conflict as something other people do, or we experience, and miss the fact, that it is also an *interaction*; a process, a relationship, and a question we are asked and can only answer with our lives, based on who we are or are prepared to become. It is this *relational* aspect of conflict that allows all of us to turn aggression, defensiveness, and avoidance into opportunities to become better human beings. *Being Relational* offers sound and practical advice on how each of us can do so, and help make ourselves and the world a little better."

—**Kenneth Cloke**, mediator and author of *The Dance of Opposites* and *Conflict Revolution*

"Knowing how the Senfts approach conflict and its transformation, I have faith that these methods can—and do—enact change. They have been used throughout our state for complex litigation, business and family matters. *Being Relational* contains a useful and commonsense formula that will work for us all."

—**Robert M. Bell**, chief judge of the Court of Appeals of Maryland and former chair of the Maryland Alternative Dispute Resolution Commission

"In an era where adults over 65 will outnumber almost every age cohort, more guidance is needed to support the transitioning process—getting Dad to give up his car keys, helping Mom decide when it's time to sell the family home and distribute family assets, or determining what health procedures make the most sense to name but a few. Along comes an unexpected instructional resource, *Being Relational*, that provides a lovingly written, comprehensive guide to change the quality of your life with beloved family members (among others). In their stunning portrait of relational living strategies and techniques, Louise Phipps Senft and William Senft invite us to become differently engaged, grounded, generous, and kind. What would seem an impossible challenge to unlearn our previous negotiating strategies for what we want, instead becomes an intuitive reference point for transformative thinking, doing, and living. *Being Relational* could not have arrived at a better time to help families change and support themselves."

—**John K. Holton, Ph.D.**, director of the Center for Gerontology at Concordia University Chicago and former director of the Illinois Department on Aging

"Having spent the past decade working across time zones and different cultures in both my professional and personal life, Louise Phipps Senft and William Senft have approached how we connect with one another in seven simple ways. In an era where we focus on diversity, work/life balance, global responsibility, and even how to adapt to a millennial work force and world, it comes down to a need for dialogue and how to do that well for positive outcomes. There is a relational leader in each of us! I am recommending *Being Relational* for all my teams and my family."

—**Loretto Kane** at Microsoft Corporation

"Being Relational brings us back to the basics, but with tremendous nuance, outlining a series of simple, yet profound, principles that will most certainly lead you to greater success. A well thought-out tutorial that centers you on your true self, focusing on caring for others yet with effective intellectual honesty."

—**James A.C. Kennedy,**
CEO at T. Rowe Price

"Being Relational is a guide for anyone who seeks to convert a lonely individual failure into an inspiring collective success. Human nature will seem less complicated after you put the book down."

—**Bob Kerrey,** *managing director at Allen and Company, co-chair of Issue One Advisory Board, and former U.S. Senator and 35th Governor of Nebraska (D)*

"Whether it's in politics, business, or simply interacting with our next-door neighbors, we're good at expressing our own views and not so good at hearing—and considering—somebody else's perspective. We have many contacts but few real interactive relationships. The result is division and conflict. This marvelous book identifies clear, effective steps that will make our relationships better and in the process lead to better outcomes for us all individually and collectively. I highly recommend it."

—**Mickey Edwards,** *former U.S. Congressman (R-OK) and vice president of the Aspen Institute*

"Being Relational provides a powerful path to one of life's treasures: ***meaningful relationships.*** Whether interacting with family, friends, business associates, or adversaries, strong relationships should be part of the outcome and the Senfts eloquently guide us there."

—**Ron Shapiro,** *chairman of Shapiro Negotiations Institute and New York Times bestselling author*

"In our fast-paced, digitally connected world, Louise and William remind us of the importance of personal interaction at the human level. Using the tools offered in ***Being Relational,*** I've seen a marked improvement in my interactions with others both in business and at home, and am introducing the concept to my teams."

—**Dan Taylor,** *director of Global Display at Google*

"It was a joy to read ***Being Relational*** after using these concepts and techniques for many years to train tribal community mediators and to mediate intra-tribal conflicts in my home community on the Hopi Reservation. ***Being Relational*** lays out the basic concepts in a clear and easy to follow format and is invaluable information for one's personal growth as well as for honing one's skills as a mediator or even just to be a responsible member of one's community. In a world where we are all expected to compete and become 'winners,' it is a relief to hear a message that, in order for any one of us to truly win, we will need to listen to each other and to care about each other to do it."

—**Patricia Sekaquaptewa,** *justice of the Hopi Appellate Court and assistant professor of the Department of Alaska Native Studies and Rural Development at the University of Alaska Fairbanks*

CHANGE THE INTERACTION, CHANGE THE OUTCOME

IN THEIR WORK as conflict negotiators and mediators, and in their personal lives as a married couple, Louise Phipps Senft and William Senft have learned that every interaction is a negotiation, and that the critical issues for us as human beings are how we negotiate, how we connect, and how we relate. Still, people are often transactional instead of relational—maximizing their own self-interests over another's. It is much more difficult to undo what you've already said, done, or not done, which can lead to struggles and stalemates. Living in an increasingly crowded and hyper-connected world, how we negotiate—and more importantly, who we are as we negotiate with others—is at the root of our desperate realities and our conflicts large and small.

Now, in this thought-provoking yet practical work rooted in teachings from many sources—conflict transformation, negotiation ethics, neuroscience, multiple faith traditions, and numerous self-help and business books, Being Relational explores the seven ways to quality interaction that anchor us:

- BEING ENGAGED
- BEING CENTERED
- BEING GROUNDED
- BEING CLEAR
- BEING GENEROUS
- BEING HUMBLE
- BEING KIND

By understanding what it really means to live these principles—much more than meets the eye —you'll also discover practical skills that will provide you with a positive mindset. You'll learn how to: effectively deal with conflict in the office; teach your children to be relational even in the age of nonstop texting and Snapchat; defuse a bully with quality engagement; reach "across the aisle" to those with opposing political viewpoints; and more. By following the comprehensive approach the Senfts have used in their practice, you will discover how quality interactions can positively impact your daily life as you—and those with whom you interact—become happier, healthier, and more content.

Louise Phipps Senft and William Senft are business and law professors, non-profit executives, mediators, lawyers, entrepreneurs, and parents of five children. For two decades, Louise has been on the faculty of the University of Maryland School of Law as well as a lecturer at Harvard Law School's Program on Negotiation, Insight Initiative. In over 20 years of experience at their firm Baltimore Mediation—one of the first alternative dispute resolution firms in the U.S.—they have gained a unique perspective on the ways that leaders and others manage conflict, experience conflict, manage themselves in conflict, solve problems, build relationships, and make their way in the world.

ORANS

BEING RELATIONAL

The Seven Ways to Quality Interaction & Lasting Change

Louise Phipps Senft
William Senft

To Dodo and Paula, Peggy and Dan,
without whom we wouldn't exist.
We love you.

To Paula, Pete, Dewey, Archer, and Dutch,
and to all of our mediation clients, you taught us
everything about quality interaction.
You inspire us every day.

To Larry Hoover and Nancy Good,
you opened the door to work in conflict transformation
for us and taught us so much about quality teaching.
We are forever grateful.

To Frank Pugh and Lily Hunn,
you taught us everything about generosity,
humility, and kindness. Pray for us and please tap us
on the shoulder when we go astray!

Contents

Introduction

Our world is a crowded and hyper-connected place and it is becoming more crowded and hyper-connected every minute. With continuous messaging through media outlets emphasizing conflict and desperately competing for our attention, our world seems full of struggles over resources and power and struggles between competing beliefs and ideologies. We are living in a time of turmoil between religious groups, greater political polarization, intractable impasse in Congress, greater gaps between haves and have-nots, greater divisions within families, cultural preference of divorce over reconciliation, and escalating conflict on the streets of our cities. The challenges of our world call us to evolve as a species in ways that never before have been necessary: not in our physical attributes, not in our emotional capacities, not in our mental capabilities, and arguably not even in our use of technology to master the environment and harness its resources. But rather, the challenges of our world call us to evolve in the ways that we *relate* to each other as fellow inhabitants of Earth and, by extension, how we relate to all living things on our planet.

In a crowded and hyper-connected world, *interaction with other people is constant* in your daily experience. It takes place in many forms—face-to-face, phone, letter, press release, media reports, email, Facebook, Twitter, Snapchat, Instagram, YouTube, and so on. It takes place on many levels: person-to-person (one-to-one), person-to-group, group-to-group, political party-to-political party, government-to-government.

Every interaction is a negotiation. You might not think of it as a negotiation when you are in it, but fundamentally, when you act or communicate in any way that affects another person, you are negotiating with them. You are seeking to affect and influence their behavior or perception of you, and whether you connect with them or not; often they, in turn, are seeking to affect and influence your behavior, your connection or perception of them, as well. Many of your interactions may seem trivial, purely in the nature of simple exchanges of information or money for goods, but they are negotiations nonetheless—and your most intimate exchanges, though you might refer to them as conversations, these too are negotiations.

How we negotiate, and more importantly, who we *are* as we negotiate life with others, is at the root of our desperate realities and our conflicts large and small.

The critical issue for us as a species is *how* we negotiate, how we connect, how we relate. The premise of this book is that how we negotiate, and more importantly, who we *are* as we negotiate life with others, is at the root of our desperate realities and our conflicts large and small. It also is the source of a great hope we have for the future and a way we can thrive in our crowded and hyper-connected planet. However, in this time of conflict, improvement in our ways of interaction is not only a hope and dream for the future, but an urgent need now.

So is this just another book on negotiation or conflict resolution? There are hundreds—many written by great scholars who have spent their careers studying the dynamics of negotiation and conflict. How can this book add to and advance your understanding?

The ways that we call *Being Relational* is a collection drawn from many sources, some familiar, some more obscure, that have come to us in twenty years of immersion in the study of conflict, the human experience of conflict, personal reactivity, and human interaction. We also owe a great deal to the thousands of people who have come to Baltimore Mediation's conflict transformation trainings that Louise has taught since 1994 and all of the insight and experience they have shared in those trainings. We can't claim that everything we offer is an original idea—how could it be? We do believe we can share a unique collection with a unique focus—on what happens in human interaction. Elements of some very popular and widely respected teachings are part of being relational, from Stephen Covey's *Seven Habits* and Fisher and Ury's *Getting to Yes*, to Bush and Folger's *The Promise of Mediation* and the Old Testament *Ten Commandments*. Our goal is not to invent some radically new idea, but rather to provide a synthesis of many ideas already out there, to organize them into a comprehensive approach that you as a reader can draw upon and

Our goal is not to invent some radically new idea, but rather to provide a synthesis of many ideas already out there, to organize them into a comprehensive approach that you as a reader can draw upon and use, check in on and grow into, as a way of being in relation to others.

use, check in on and grow into, as a way of being in relation to others—something akin to *Ignatian Spirituality* of Catholic Jesuits and the *Buddha Dharma*—but focused exclusively on ***how*** *you interact with others and how* ***who you are*** *affects how you interact.*

Our hope is that the relational ways offered in this book will make you and those you interact with happier, healthier, and more content—because of the quality of the interactions you have and the impact your way of being has on you and on others.

Our belief is that through widespread adoption of relational ways, together we can increase well-being and create lasting positive change for ourselves, for our families, and for our planet.

Desperate Realities

We want to share with you something that has emerged for us through the years of our professional practice as mediators, and through our family life with five children living in the bubble of prosperity that is the East Coast of the United States. Something that we hear echoed every day in so many voices on Facebook, Twitter, in blogs, in lectures we hear on radio, in YouTube videos, in the multitude of self-help books, and even in magazines we read in the checkout line at the supermarket. *Despite our great prosperity in America, especially on the East and West Coasts, there is a restlessness, an emptiness, and confusion.* Millions are struggling to find a peaceful and fulfilling life for themselves and those they love. For too many, the way of life that we have held as the standard for so long is not working and in many ways it is toxic to the health of our souls and to the soul of our global family.

We all live in different realities. For too many, a desperate reality is their daily experience. Poverty, lack of education, disease, and disability are just a few of the root causes of this despair. Some of these causes are completely out of our collective control, but *much of what brings on suffering that can lead to despair can be affected, ameliorated, by the actions and choices of those who live in health and wealth. The choices made by those blessed few, the "winners," affect every person in our society.*

Let's clarify what we mean by "winner" here. If you are someone who has many advantages in life—success or a clear path to it, an investment account, comfort, leisure time—we know you. We want this book to have meaning for you. Your success, or winning, has likely been achieved through a blend of hard work and discipline, plus advantages of the family and socioeconomic class you were born into. But regardless of the path to it, you have a life that others might only wish for. So your reality is a good one—right?

Maybe, maybe not. Living in a desperate reality is not exclusively reserved for the poor and less fortunate. Those of us who are blessed to live in America with health and wealth know from experience; we too may live with despair or feel its presence as it lurks just outside of our experience. We see flashes of it in our lives, and as we encounter it, often many times a day, we must make the *conscious choices* needed to create the different reality that our nature craves—the reality of joy, abundance and love, not just for ourselves, but also for others.

> We must make the *conscious choices* needed to create the different reality that our nature craves—the reality of joy, abundance and love, not just for ourselves, but also for others.

This book is about those choices and for each of us, choosing a different reality might mean a radical change.

In the upper economic levels of American society, the desperate reality of life in a society that is ultra-competitive, where escalating lifestyle expectations drive desperate behavior, may have touched your experience. This reality has many dark and empty dimensions—from isolation, to insecurity and dissatisfaction in the face of success, to feelings of emptiness—despite the material abundance it springs from. It's certainly not pleasant to think about and perhaps you are thinking, "Thank God that's not my reality!" *But maybe there is a piece of it that* ***is*** *part of your reality.* Maybe it is worth considering why that is so. Maybe you want to do something to change your story, to change your reality. Maybe not. You have options. You can make different choices—in what you do, in what you say, in what you think. This book is about those choices.

We are not going to make the argument here in these pages that there is a problem by offering statistics and anecdotes to prove that our winning way of life is producing desperate realities. Others have done that and better than we can. We *know* that there is a problem, and we invite you to explore ways to address the problem, even if you *don't* believe there is a problem and you are happy and secure in your life and your world just the way it is.

ORANS

Part One:

What Is Your Approach to Interaction?

Twenty Years of Immersion in Conflict Transformation

The past twenty years of our professional careers have been devoted to the study of negotiation, teaching negotiation, and facilitating others in negotiation as mediators. In our work as mediators, we have spent much more than the requisite 10,000 hours (see Malcolm Gladwell's *Outliers*) with people locked in difficult conflict: inviting them to dialogue, working to improve the quality of their interactions, and helping bring about shifts in perspective from weakness and self-absorption to strength and recognition of the other. Our experience in this crucible, sitting in the fire as we and others would say in the field of conflict resolution, has brought us a unique perspective on how people relate to each other and how they find their way through very difficult times—even extreme situations where the threat of violence is real, where the use of power and intimidation is not subtle but explicit, and where rational thought is trampled beneath powerful emotion and mental instability.

This book offers the best of what we have learned as mediators, what we have learned and observed about being relational, namely how we, individually and collectively, can relate in a way that is good for us, for others, and for our world. And so, while we firmly believe and teach that good practice comes from a solid foundation of theory, we want this book to provide you with practical and familiar anchoring concepts and associated skills

> We want this book to provide you with practical and familiar anchoring concepts and associated skills and practices—what being relational *means* and *how* to be relational.

and practices—what being relational *means* and *how* to be relational—and we want to connect with you and influence you to choose a relational approach. Going forward, as you make those daily choices, we want to help you **grow into being relational as your natural way of being**. We don't just want you to *know* about being relational; we want to help you along the path to the place where being relational is you authentically being you. Being relational in practice may dramatically change your life.

ORANS

Chapter 1

Being Transactional—A Way that Works for Winners?

The problem is what might be called a transactional approach to our interactions with others—our negotiations—acting to serve our needs and desires and placing little value on the quality of interaction with the other person and their well-being—all those moments in our lives when we choose to try to get the best of the situation at the expense of others or to the disregard of others. A transactional approach views interactions with others as transactions where the goal is to get the maximum value for oneself. But let's be clear, we are not

A transactional approach views interactions with others as transactions where the goal is to get the maximum value for oneself.

claiming that self-interest, and the competitive drive that serves it, is inherently unhealthy. In fact, it is unquestionably good. But when it becomes a way of life and governs all our interactions and how we view our place in the world, then it leads to undesirable outcomes, needless suffering, and a cycle of festering or escalating conflict.

Maximizing Self-Interest—A Rational Choice

Many aspects of the world today reward and encourage a transactional approach. We can get away with much in the way of self-interested behavior, including the maximum self-interested behavior that spurs us to be intimidating and deceptive. Ironically, in a world with billions of people living in it, side-by-side or connected through the Internet, we lose sight of the individual, personal side of the interaction. It might seem that no one really cares or that no one is really looking, so, "Who cares?" As if we are all anonymous actors with no connection to anyone else except those closest to us. After all, when we interact with another person in many, if not most, circumstances we can assume that we will never deal with them again and that their well-being is irrelevant to ours.

When faced with a choice of how to act in relation to a person whom we assume we will never deal with again, a coldly rational, logical choice would be to do whatever maximizes our self-interest, "I'll never see him again, so . . ." In these anonymous interactions, the relationship with that other person is of no value and not a consideration. It's like we are economists, weighing risk and return, and making a calculation to gain as much as possible.

And it's not just how we approach our interactions with those we encounter on a daily basis. When we see the suffering and need of others, we can give thanks that it's not ours and feel pity, but nothing compels us personally to take responsibility to act to alleviate that suffering. A transactional approach makes government and charities responsible to care for those with unmet needs. The responsibility of good citizens is to maximize earnings, consume goods and services as desired, pay taxes as required by law, and give money to those charities that are appealing. So what's wrong with that? That's the American system. It's efficient and it has worked for more than 200 years.

Competition and Winning

Fundamentally, a transactional approach is based on competition. It's a competitive world, compete to get what you want and let the other guy compete to get what he wants—that's fair right? Make it fair, but may the best man or woman win. The concept of relating to another in a competitive way is at the core of a winner. After all, a winner becomes a winner by competing and . . . winning. What would a game be without competition? Without a winner there is no game at all; the competition is what makes it fun.

Competition makes us better. It keeps us on the run. There is always someone competing with us, ready to take our place, so we are insecure and always striving. The striving, the struggle, makes us stronger and smarter. Without competition we become lazy, self-indulgent, and weak. Winners are hard-working, disciplined, and strong. These, no doubt, are admirable qualities and the winners deserve whatever rewards they can manage to gain from their efforts. You're a winner. You know the benefits.

Winning is defined as consistent success in life's series of transactions, resulting in a winner's accumulation of wealth, prestige, and the means to pursue comfort and pleasure.

Winning is defined as consistent success in life's series of transactions, resulting in a winner's accumulation of wealth, prestige, and the means to pursue comfort and pleasure. This definition is reinforced by almost all of the most influential structures in our society—*our schools*, placing us in competition with other students to gain admission to top universities; *our universities*, measuring student and faculty value according to metrics in comparison to peer institutions, aggressively courting and placing wealthy donors on a pedestal; *our media*, delivering images and messages to us to spur our consumption of goods and services so we can feel more secure and judge ourselves favorably in lifestyle terms in comparison to others; and *our government*, setting our societal goals in terms of growth in the economy through winning in the global marketplace.

Competition results in elevating the best and the brightest among us to create greater innovation, better technology, longer lifespans, and an efficient allocation of the scarce resources of our planet. Who can argue that competition is not a way of interaction that results in positive outcomes—a fair way to create the most good for the most people. It's our way of life. Right?

Scarcity

From a transactional point of view, competition is grounded in the perceived reality of scarcity—scarcity in resources, scarcity in time. There isn't enough of what we want to go around. Not everyone can go to Harvard. Not everyone can have a nice house. Not everyone can be the CEO. Not everyone can retire in comfort and leisure. Not every nation can have a high standard of living. It's Economics 101. There is only one fair way to decide who gets what they want and who doesn't—through competition. What other way is there?

For the winners, it's a chosen way of life. The irony is that the perceived reality of scarcity creates insecurity. Be the best in everything you do. Establish yourself as a winner, or be ready to face hardship, humiliation, and death—winding up sick, poor, and alone. You can give back when you make it, when you have everything you need and desire and you feel secure that all your days will be lived in comfort and security. Until then, get as much as you can as fast as you can because you never know when the next guy might come along and take your spot. It's survival of the fittest. That's the way it is has been since the dawn of time, and it is healthy and good for the evolution of mankind.

Profits

Part of winning in a transactional approach is not only maximizing gain in each transaction, but also creating highly efficient systems to maximize the gain of organizations—profits.

Companies, with power concentrated in the hands of owners who demand a focus on profitability and growth, maximize gain by doing everything possible to employ human resources at the optimum balance of lowest cost and highest productivity. In some instances, this means making compromises in safety, quality, and environmental stewardship, as well as a wide variety of unethical practices. In addition, in case you were wondering, nonprofits also work to maximize gain by focusing great energies on fundraising, building endowments, growing in facilities, and expanding programs—"biggering" as Dr. Seuss would call it in his famous book *The Lorax*. Government works to maximize gain in the same way by continually expanding the scope of its services, programs and regulations and by taxing to fund its growth. Nations maximize gain, not only through the old-fashioned methods of conquest and colonization, but through expanding influence using economic and military power.

Power

And that last little word, right there at the end of the last paragraph, is what is at the core of a transactional approach founded on competition—***power***. It can come from a number of sources—physical strength and ability to inflict harm, superior technology and know-how, deeper financial resources, greater human resources, and better access to information and intelligence—to name just a few. A transactional approach is power based. Those with more power, from whatever source, will win and can maximize their gain in dealings with others resulting in the greater and greater accumulation of power by those who have it.

A transactional approach is power based.

Many structures exist to *limit* the exercise of power—for instance, alliances between those with less power to gain strength and laws protecting against violence, fraud and exploitation. A society organized around a transactional approach makes those structures essential to prevent pandemic chaos and misery. But, as we see in the news reports daily, those structures created to limit the exercise of power too often fail and leave too many people behind in the wake of the expanding prosperity and power of the winners. We also know that power-based solutions in conflicts between groups of people—wars, both hot and cold—only perpetuate and escalate conflict.

The challenge for those who are the winners—the ones with the power and for whom this book was written—and the hope for our evolution is to change the paradigm of interaction. Looking closely at how we use our power, compete, negotiate, and relate, the shift from being transactional to being relational can begin, and we can ***move from focusing only on self and maximizing gain, to focusing on both self and other and maximizing well-being.***

ORANS

Chapter 2

Being Relational—The Seven Ways

So what does it mean to be relational? It can be reduced to seven ways of being:

Being Engaged
Being Centered
Being Grounded
Being Clear
Being Generous
Being Humble
Being Kind

Now you might look at this list and think, "Well, I might as well put this book down now because I already know all about these things." But we invite you to keep going. Why? Because each of these anchoring concepts, each of these seven ways of being, has a ***much more than meets the eye*** quality. Each can be understood on a glib, surface level (*Hey, I'm not stupid; I know what it means to be kind!*), but much is revealed when these concepts are cracked open and unpacked. Each has implications going well beyond familiar cliché platitudes like "Go with the flow" and "It is what it is." Each has importance in every significant relationship in your life. Each greatly affects how much you suffer and experience internal turmoil and how you affect the suffering and internal turmoil of others. Each represents a crossroad on your path to either a desperate reality or a reality of well-being for yourself and others.

Being Conscious and Deliberate in Your Choices

As you make choices about what you do or don't do, what you say or don't say, what you support or oppose, in each instance you may or may not ***be relational***. By fully exploring these seven ways, you will become more conscious and deliberate in the choices that you make. For many people, the processes of interaction are automatic, based on habits governing reactions (or lack thereof) to various situations, and based on learned behavior influenced by any number of sources including family, society, media, attachment, nurturing, trauma, love, approval, rejection, insecurity, and many more. Our goal is to help you become more intentional in the choices you make. Being relational *can* become a way of being for you, but it will never be an automatic habit. It will always require an exercise of

For many people, the processes of interaction are automatic.

your free will. You may decide that one or more of the ***seven ways of being*** explored in this book are "just not me" or "just don't fit with my experience" or "just seem too (insert adjective here) for me," but, having taken a 360 degree look at them, after reading this book you will be able to say that your choices are *intentional* and *deliberate*—**your** choices, based on your more fully informed decisions about what you believe is right and best in how you act in relation to others. And, as you continue to make these choices daily, you may discover a new way of being, not only a new set of behaviors and attitudes that you can put on like a new set of clothes, but a new *you*—a you that is naturally and authentically relational, a you that is healthier and more content, a you that empowers and brings joy to yourself and others. So . . . keep going. Winners have stamina.

> Influenced by any number of sources including family, society, media, attachment, nurturing, trauma, love, approval, rejection, insecurity, and many more. Our goal is to help you become more intentional in the choices you make.

Ways That Are Universally Applicable

Another question you might be asking is "Why these seven?" When we say ***relational*** many things may come to your mind; many words may be associated with your concept of relating to another person in a healthy way—words like *cooperative, collaborative, open,* and *trusting.* Aren't these part of being relational? Why aren't they part of the seven ways? The answer is that, yes, they are part of being relational and, no, they are not left out. For example, being relational involves a combination of attitudes and behaviors that often will be cooperative, *but not always.* There are times when cooperation is completely inappropriate in being relational toward another, such as when they threaten harm or use power to exploit and oppress. And the same can be said with being collaborative, open, and trusting.

These explain *positive* ways that you are in relation to another, but do not universally apply to the way you relate, especially in conflict. These concepts imply a level of alignment with another or at least a neutral posture toward the other. That may be the case in the vast majority of your interactions, but clearly not always. These positive ways are aspirational—ways that you may hope to be in positive relationship with another. In contrast, it is always relational to be engaged, centered, grounded, and clear—ways of being that prevent conflict from escalating and promote quality interaction. *In addition, it is always relational to be generous, humble, and kind—ways of being that create positive outcomes which reverberate, are paid forward, and foster reconciliation, peace, well-being, and lasting and positive change. But these ways do not imply any alignment with another.* These seven ways are universally applicable, within your control, and involve choices always available to you in how you relate to friends or enemies, to those you know well and to those who are strangers and everyone in between, including all of the anonymous others with whom you interact. Yes, you can be relational even when you have no ***relationship***. Yes, you can be relational even when facing violence and dealing with those who are in no way being relational toward you—even terrorists.

It is always relational to be engaged, centered, grounded, and clear—ways of being that prevent conflict from escalating and promote quality interaction.

Roles Affecting Your Ways of Being Relational

And, just as there are many orientations that others have in their dealings with you—supporting you, alongside you, coming at you, pursuing you, moving away from you, indifferent or neutral to you—so too, do you find yourself in many different roles when you interact with others. First, obviously, you act on your own behalf. But often, you act on behalf of another person—such as when you are an employee or agent for another person or organization. Sometimes you are in the middle of someone else's conflict. We have a great deal of experience with that, serving formally as mediators engaged to intervene and work with others in conflict. But, even if you are not a professional mediator, you often act informally in what we call a "little m" mediator role—at home, in the workplace, and in your community. Sometimes you are alongside others in a group, as a teammate, or member of a family, clan, or tribe. Sometimes you are in a position of authority over others as a boss, manager, committee chair, or elected position holder; sometimes others are in a position of authority over you. In all of these roles you can be relational, but how you are relational will look different depending on your role. For each of the seven ways of being relational, we will explore how your role in a particular situation affects your choices in how you relate and how you influence the way others relate to you.

For each of the seven ways of being relational, we will explore how your role in a particular situation affects your choices in how you relate and how you influence the way others relate to you.

Lastly, in looking at the seven ways, it is also important to note that, while each attitude and set of behaviors is distinct, the lines between them are quite blurry. They mix into each other and blend like the colors in a spectrum of light, a rainbow. But despite the blurry lines, together these ways constitute the full spectrum of what it means to be relational. So we will look at each individually, but we will keep in mind that all of these ways of being are involved in every interaction—or not—depending on the choices you make in the moment. So let's take a closer look at those choices.

ORANS

Part Two:

The Four Ways to Quality Interaction

You have the power to change the quality of your interaction with others. As a winner, you often meet others in a position of advantage or relative strength in relation to them, and with that strength comes the ability to influence how the interaction proceeds. And, even if you find yourself in a situation where your posture in relation to another is equal or subordinate, you still can greatly influence how the interaction takes place by how you respond to that person.

How will you relate to the other person? How will you respond to how they relate to you? In being relational, your first priority is to focus on the quality of the interaction with the other person. This brings the first four ways of being relational into play: **Being Engaged, Being Centered, Being Grounded** and **Being Clear**. These four ways lead to quality dialogue. They tend not to escalate conflict in an unhealthy way. They are based in the transformative theory of conflict that is foundational to our mediation practice. Twenty years of experience have taught us that this theory provides great insight into what people value most in their interactions.

In being relational, your first priority is to focus on the quality of the interaction with the other person.

Transformative Theory of Conflict[1]

Instinctively you know that good negotiation—quality dialogue, healthy interaction—does not involve a degree of conflict that you experience as destructive. It does not involve conflict that drives a lasting wedge of ill will between you and the other person. It does not degenerate into name-calling, stonewalling or worse, a situation where people view each other as bad, evil, or even, at the extreme, less than human. The Transformative Theory of Conflict explains that negative and destructive conflict is not simply a problem to be solved, but rather is a crisis in interaction that profoundly affects how you feel about yourself and how you feel about others when you are in the midst of it. If you are interested in learning more about this theory and the corresponding skill set for mediating, you can attend a Transformative Mediation and Conflict Transformation Skills training, ours or one offered by the Institute on Conflict Transformation.

At the root of what makes conflict escalate and dialogue deteriorate in a destructive spiraling cycle are two distinct experiences of conflict. First, you feel *weakness* in some form, such as: you are losing control, you are confused about your options, you don't know how to respond to the way that the other person is coming at you, you question your own ability to manage the situation, you can't make a decision and stick with it, you are frustrated, you feel like you are grasping at straws to find solutions, or you are losing confidence and hope of preventing a bad outcome. Second, you become *self-absorbed*, such as: you are suspicious of the other, you

1 See Bush & Folger, *The Promise of Mediation* (2nd Ed. 2005). This is the seminal work in the field of transformative theory and mediation.

are making negative assumptions about the other's motives and morality, you are guarding and protecting yourself from a perceived threat, you shut down your curiosity about the other, or you are so focused on your own suffering and weakness that you are unable to consider the other person's perspective.

Theory of Relational Reciprocity

The experience of weakness and self-absorption feeds a cycle that escalates conflict. For instance, the more closed you are to understanding the other person's perspective, the more suspicious you become; the more suspicious you are, the more fearful you become; the more fearful you are, the more angry you become; and on and on. To Transformative Conflict Theory, we would add a theory we've developed and seen borne out over and over in our more than twenty years of practice in mediation, the theory of relational reciprocity. This theory states that there is a physical energy created and expended in the ways we choose to relate to each other. Each intention and action creates energy. When in conflict, the more suspicious and angry energy you have with another person, the weaker and more self-absorbed experience they will have with you. This reciprocity can manifest itself in different ways, including when the other person shuts down mentally and emotionally, with an equal and opposing energetic intensity. The response of the other person may not be the exact same as yours, but it will manifest with the same amount of energy. So, the more frustrated you are, the more closed they become. The more closed you are to them, the more forceful they become to you. The Transformative Theory of Conflict and our theory of relational reciprocity both posit that you are not doomed to remain in this negative and destructive cycle. You have both the *capacity* to change the interaction and a powerful innate *motivation* to restore your sense of connectedness to the other person. Even in the midst of bitter conflict, you have the ability, springing from your essential strength and empathy, to be engaged, centered, grounded, and clear. You call upon this strength instinctively because of the moral and social impulse that is your genetic birthright and is within your very soul. And according to the theory of relational reciprocity, the more you act relationally by fostering your inner strength to be engaged, centered, grounded, and clear, the more the other person will respond relationally to you.

You have both the *capacity* to change the interaction and a powerful innate *motivation* to restore your sense of connectedness.

A Focus on Interaction

Following the theories, those attitudes and practices that help you remain calm, confident, and clear, as well as open, empathic, and attentive, lead to quality interaction—good negotiation. In the midst of the escalating spiral of conflict, these same attitudes and practices can help you shift from relatively weak to stronger and shift from relatively self-absorbed to more responsive to the other person, bringing on what Bush and Folger refer to as Empowerment and Recognition shifts.

Those attitudes and practices that help you remain calm, confident, and clear, as well as open, empathic, and attentive, lead to quality interaction—good negotiation.

Furthermore, these ways also have great potential to affect the way that the other person experiences you and the way that they relate to you—building a positive, constructive cycle of interaction. So how do you do that? You focus on the quality of interaction. You focus on the interaction itself. You bring to your interactions the Seven Ways of Being Relational, starting with the four fundamental attitudes and practices of conflict transformation: Being Engaged, Being Centered, Being Grounded, and Being Clear. Let's explore what each of these means and the ***more than meets the eye*** quality to each of them.

ORANS

Chapter 3

Being Engaged

Common sense tells you that you can't interact, you can't negotiate, you can't have a conversation, you can't relate to another person unless you engage with them. It is the *sine qua non*, the first thing involved in being relational. But so often you don't engage. Habitually or unconsciously you may exhibit one of the following behaviors:

- You avoid the uncomfortable subject or avoid the other entirely.
- You are sleepy, mentally idle, or disinterested in other people.
- You are distracted, preoccupied with some other thought, thing, or stimulus.
- You are present, but closed to any other perspective than your own.
- You are rigid and impenetrable: you stonewall others.
- You are impulsive and strike out to push other people away, to crush or swat others aside.

To be engaged, we invite you to focus on the quality of the interaction itself. Take a close look, a micro-focused look, at daily interactions. Take a look at how you interact with other people. If you regularly, habitually, fall into any of the above behaviors and coping strategies, you are not engaged. These may be habits that protect you, but they are barriers to engagement with others. You can change that if you want to.

This is an opportunity to become conscious of the choices you make when you are not engaged. You can pause. Take a breath. Activate your self-observer. Observe your behavior coming on. Use that part of your consciousness that is able to look at your patterns, your habitual way of proceeding, to discern your path more deliberately. Make space internally for the energy of your thought patterns and feelings before you move into action. Locate where they show up in your body with a brief body scan. Pause to be curious about that place inside your body where the energy of your habit manifests somatically. Make mental note of it, be curious about it, attend to it. Then shift your attention to a different part of your body that is not activated. This will provide you with a fresh physical resource. Now shift your attention back again to the place in your body that is tight or reactive, feel your habitual ways asserting themselves. Feel them affecting your body. Give yourself space on the inside for this physical quality to calm down before acting out of habit, exercising a sort of forbearance that comes from the discipline of a focus that allows a relaxation of your habits of mind. This is a centering practice that we will discuss in greater depth later, but you may need to be aware of your own personal reactivity before you engage with another. For you see, being relational is not a sequential process. It is not a step one, step two kind of thing. Being relational is being all seven ways at once, with each way coming to the front of your consciousness in different moments as you discern your path. Being relational can also mean being just one of the ways at any given moment in time. For instance, you may have many experiences where it is simply enough to be self-aware as you engage.

Being relational is being all seven ways at once, with each way coming to the front of your consciousness in different moments as you discern your path.

So, when you have shifted your mental attention internally and provided oxygen to your body and to your brain from intentional breath work before acting out of habit, you are more focused and you are now able to engage. Engaging is a deliberate act. It is an act of ease once practiced, but it is never habitual. It takes commitment to be engaged and live relationally. The acknowledgment of another, pausing in your life to be fully with another even for a second, is such a simple act, yet it can take so much awareness and courage to do it. You know how to be engaged; you do it all of the time when it's comfortable and you want to. Much of it is common sense, but ask—am I aware of my habits when I am on autopilot? When I am in a difficult situation? It is those times that provide the greatest opportunity to take a close look at your behaviors, change some habits, and establish new ones so that you can be engaged more than you ever have been. You may need terminology—some words to hold in your consciousness to anchor you and remind you to be engaged. Words like *present, attentive,* and *interested.*

Being Engaged Is Being Present

You have had the experience of talking to another and you just know they do not hear a word you are saying. They are not present and their non-presence triggers a habitual conflict response in you. Being present means that you are physically, mentally, emotionally, right there *with* the other person. You know when someone is present with you and reciprocally they know when you are present with them. It takes effort. Your effort is an act of generosity on your part, giving of yourself. Being relational means you do it anyway, even if there is apparently no gain to be had for yourself in doing it, nor any discernable reciprocity from the other in that moment. Being relational means you do it anyway because you believe in the benefits it will provide to yourself and to the other person.

You are ready to offer a genuine smile and let others know that you see them; they are not invisible. A simple nod, eye connection, and "Good afternoon." This includes your colleagues when you walk down the hallway at work, your housemate or your family when you walk in the front door, tired as you might be after a long day, "Hello everyone! I'm home. How is everybody?" Or if you are the one at home, preoccupied or not, in a different part of the house or not, and a family member enters through the front door, you say "Hi, son!" or "Hi, sweetheart!" And it includes an obnoxious ex-spouse or a sour-puss neighbor, "Hello, Charlie." Yes, it takes effort. When you give it, whether returned or not in that moment, there is a quality of dignity and honoring of self and other, we are both important. We inhabit the same space, the same planet. It matters and, as we are beginning to understand through quantum physics, it shifts energy positively—relational reciprocity.

In choosing to be present, you prefer face-to-face. You take the time to visit with someone rather than just sending a message. You use email and texts for routine factual and supportive messages, but you don't use them to engage in any important discussion with another person, especially if there is an emotional component or a difference that emerges. If you can't meet in person, you pick up the phone and make a call. You know that firing email and text messages back and forth, though it feels safe, only escalates conflict. The illusion of safety is false. So much is lost when communication is not in person—tone of voice, eye contact, gestures, body language, and the intangible yet potent quality of just being in the presence of another human being.

Being present means you show up. Your face is in the place. You have the courage and you put in the effort to get yourself physically there to interact with the other person. You also take care of yourself so that you can be physically present—avoiding excess in drink, and making sure to get the sleep you need, for instance. You don't make yourself sick with the lifestyle you lead, being hard on yourself by shoveling in a diet of too much or too little—too much food, too little food, too much medication, too much high living, too much work. It's hard to be engaged, present, and deeply attentive when you are in excess.

> Being present means you show up. You have the courage and you put in the effort to get yourself physically there to interact with the other person.

You don't duck out, avoid and evade. You aren't on the couch at home, or lying in bed or AWOL from work or home with some excuse because you can't deal with someone or something. You are not fading into the woodwork; you are not a wallflower. You are not pretending you are doing something else, hoping no one says anything to you or that you are not called upon. You take the phone call; you make it to the meeting—even if you fear that you might be outed or criticized, or that it might be a waste of time and you have much better things to do. In fact, you *ask* for the meeting and you work to make it happen. That makes for some long days, but you do it anyway because you are committed to being engaged.

And while you are physically present, you are also mentally present. This may be much harder. Being present mentally requires concentration. You are awake. You are alert and open to what unfolds, open to reality as it really is. You know your body and your mind and you know what you need in order to be awake. If your brain is fuzzy and you are sleepwalking through your day, you can't be engaged. This doesn't mean that you are manic, always on, wired, or hyperactive. You are awake and alert when you are with others—in a way that lets them know that you are with them, that you are present.

Being Engaged Is Being Attentive

Part of being present mentally and emotionally, in the sense of *being there* for others, is being attentive. When you are with others in a situation where you are expected to be mentally present, you make it a point to give your attention to them. Often it's easy to show up and then mentally check out and be somewhere else entirely. If you are nodding and saying "Uh-huh" reflexively, habitually, without awareness of what you are nodding and saying "Uh-huh" to, then you aren't attentive. Or if you say "Uh-huh" dismissively because you are in tunnel vision for getting what you want and the other person is just getting in your way, you aren't attentive to the other. Either way, you sow the seeds of conflict with others with your lack of attention.

If you are automatically saying "No" or reflexively thinking "That's ridiculous. Stupid. Here we go again," you also are not attentive and you are sowing the seeds of conflict with others with your lack of attention. As we will discuss ahead in Being Centered, when people feel dismissed, they will push back stronger, or go elsewhere to be against you. Keeping this in mind is good motivation for you to give others your attention in the moment of interaction. But giving others your full attention is never easy. It can drift away in a daydream or be lost in an instant as you react to a distracting stimulus. Focusing your attention is in many ways the fundamental skill of being relational. It takes mental discipline; it takes effort.

So . . . when engaged with others, you ignore your cell phone. You close your laptop, your tablet or any other device dividing your attention. Your eyes focus on others, noticing their expression, their eyes, mouth, posture, and gestures. You stop thinking. You make mental and emotional space for the other to enter your experience. You don't analyze, interpret, or prepare to respond. As Stephen Covey suggests, you seek first to understand others. As Eckhart Tolle suggests, you are in the Now. With your full attention given, you can listen to others.

Being Engaged Is Listening, Reflecting, and Asking Open Questions

As mediation and conflict transformation trainers, we have been teaching the art of listening for over two decades. Listening

> Listening isn't just a skill. Like presence, it too is more of an attitude, one of curiosity and openness.

isn't just a skill. Like presence, it too is more of an attitude, one of curiosity and openness—but there are definitely practices that can make you a better listener. First, you recognize the challenge associated with the mere process of verbal communication. Yes, your brain is processing the words and working to comprehend them, working to follow what another is trying to communicate to you, but you can lose track while processing their stream of words, and the thoughts of others may not be clear or very well expressed. Verbal communication is complex and difficult and often it simply is not done well. Not everyone can spontaneously roll out perfectly formed sentences. Indeed, most people cannot speak clearly at all, especially when you slip out of gear into the experience of conflict or challenge. The words you choose may not communicate the meaning to another that you intended. You express ideas that are not complete. So you are aware that you may fail to communicate your intended message clearly to another. Rather than blame them for not understanding, you allow for the possibility that others may not be doing any better than you are.

Leaving aside the complexity of the content you intend to communicate, the mere process of verbal communication itself is inherently messy. So more is needed to listen effectively—to understand others and to help them be understood. When others feel understood, they are more likely to be able to understand you—relational reciprocity.

As mediators, the skills associated with effective communication are our stock-in-trade. Three practices that are particularly helpful are **listening attentively**, **reflection,** and **open questions**. All three are elegantly simple, but can be hard to do. Here's how. Listen attentively: suspend what you think, feel, and want to say. Be aware of your own impulses to either: agree with, align with, give advice to, or tell others what to do; or your impulse to disagree with, dismiss, and put them down. These impulses come from your personality, your life experiences, and your own personal reactivity. They may assist you in other times in your life, but they are barriers to listening attentively. Remember relational reciprocity. There is a huge pay-off to having enough discipline to suspend your judgment and assumptions, and even your good advice. When you listen attentively, the other person will experience you in the way they most yearn for you to experience them: fully as a human being. They will be more likely to hear and experience you in the way you most desire.

To this quality of listening, add a reflection. As you listen deeply, you must focus closely on the other person's words and listen to what they are saying exactly, including their emotional expressions and intonations. When they finish their thought, reflect back both the facts and the feelings they conveyed using their exact words, not yours. Why do this? Because it shows the utmost of respect for the speaker to not get in their way. It communicates that you are with them, by their side, neither behind them nor ahead of them, honoring their story and fostering their empowerment. To reflect another in this way allows that person to edit, to change, to modify, or to retract what they were saying. It is a vehicle for clarity and understanding. When

Reflect back both the facts and the feelings they conveyed using their exact words, not yours.

clarity emerges, there is a relief—an opening, a stronger chance for mental understanding and, potentially, compassion. Your interaction is strengthened. Whether you are strangers or intimately familiar with each other, the quality of your relating to each other is strengthened.

Be sure to stay in the listening attentively mind-set and reflect back exactly what they said, without an edge or your bias or interpretation or spin. That can be very difficult if you are used to reframing others' ideas into your own words. You are not paraphrasing. You are not agreeing, advising, interpreting, or reframing. **Allow them to edit and to change what they said**. Listen deeply again and offer another reflection. Do this again. When the other person has calmed down a bit, you can then **ask an open question**: "What else is important?" "What else do you want to tell me?" "What else do you want me to know or understand?" An open question is one that does not seek a particular answer, a question that does not call for a yes or no response. It is not a leading question. It has no content agenda and is not trying to steer the conversation to what you want. Be amazed at what is said, including thank you, even from someone you thought did not like you or was your adversary. The yearning to be understood, and thus connected, is deeply hard-wired, in our cellular structure, and held by all human beings. The best part for you in choosing to be engaged is that because you also want to give of yourself to the other and are committed to the effort to do so, you now have

An open question is one that does not seek a particular answer, a question that does not call for a yes or no response. It is not a leading question. It has no content agenda and is not trying to steer the conversation to what you want.

a much better chance that the other person will now be able to listen to you. And if not right at that moment, then set a time for later, and be committed to it, because you are genuinely interested in others. You are curious.

Being Engaged Is Being Interested

Being engaged, present, and attentive involves adopting an open attitude. That open attitude is based on curiosity and interest in other people, even in casual conversation. "Tell me, how are you, and how are the kids?" "Tell me about your summer." "Tell me how your aging parents are doing." "How did the meeting go with so and so?" Or to the stranger in the next seat on the airplane, "So, where are you headed today?" Or if someone else asked you first about how you are, or about *your* life, *your* summer vacation, taking care of *your* aging parents, and so on, and you share what is on your mind, then your relational attitude of interest in the other person informs you to follow up with the same genuine inquiry to them, *"And how about for you?"* Being relational is attending to yourself **and** others. You may be thinking, *Okay, so that's nice, but isn't that just making small talk?* It may be no more than chit-chat, but it is not idle or wasted. It might be what used to be referred to as good manners. When it is intentional because we are committed to living relationally, interest in other people builds capacity through connection and civility. We are interested in and care about the quality of the interaction, however brief, with the other person. We are not just politely filling time or simply

> We are interested in and care about the quality of the interaction, however brief, with the other person.

exchanging pleasantries. We are genuinely interested and we want to create an open space for the exchange of humanity. We care about building and strengthening relationships, both old and new, in the moment, whether with someone we see regularly or with someone we will never see again. Both are equally important when living relationally.

But what about the difficult interactions? Being engaged with the person who appears to be against you? Your enemy? Your attitude of curiosity will serve you well there also. So, if it is a heated debate around the kitchen table or the board room conference table, you pause, check in within yourself, notice what is tight or pounding or racing (heart, belly, neck, head), breathe to provide new oxygen for clear thinking, then, with self-awareness and purpose, you offer your views and ask, "So what do you think about this?" or "I'm interested in why you said that." or "While I might see this differently than you do, I see you care deeply about this." or "When you say that, I want to understand why it is important to you." **You suspend your judgment of others and remain open.** Open to getting new information. Open to gaining better understanding of others. Open to looking for opportunities for empowerment and recognition shifts—based on your understanding of the Transformative Theory of Conflict. It's being strong enough to be vulnerable, open, welcoming to others, even when our viewpoints are different or our interactions are unpleasant. When you intentionally approach others in the posture of openness and receptiveness, there is a physical quality about the stance. When you are calm and strong and open, the other is much more likely to respond to you in a more positive, more relational way—building a positive, constructive cycle of interaction, relational reciprocity.

They might not respond in this way initially, but they are much more likely to if you maintain your attitude of openness and curiosity than if you do not. As for handling those who respond back to you negatively, there is more ahead on dealing with others who are not engaged in a way that promotes quality dialogue.

So, following these methods and attitudes for being engaged—being present, attentive, and interested—is critical to quality interaction. But your ability to be engaged is very much affected by your ability to avoid being sidetracked by your reactivity and your habits in aligning with others. So, now let's look at how, while you are engaged, you can also be centered.

Questions for Your Consideration

In exploring Being Engaged, consider the following questions. If you are not sure about your answers, go back and visit the chapter.

- How do you slow down a difficult conversation so that you can avoid defending and reacting?
- What is your approach when you know that someone wants to talk to you and you don't want to talk to them?
- What do you do when you get an email that upsets you?
- What do you do to make sure that you are present and attentive when you are with someone?
- How do you respond to someone who says something to you that you think is completely false or outrageous?

- What do you do when you sense that someone you care about may be angry or upset with you, but they haven't said anything to you about it?
- What reasons do you have to be interested in the life of another person if you can't imagine ever having any kind of relationship with them personally, professionally or otherwise?
- How can you show others that you are interested in them?

Chapter 4

Being Centered

If you are not centered, your ability to engage is seriously impaired and may be completely negated. Keep in mind that being relational is not a step-by-step process. It's not a do this, then do that kind of thing. In order to promote quality dialogue, you want to do your best to be engaged, centered, grounded, and clear all at the same time. You may already have a concept in your mind of what it means to be centered, maybe not, or maybe it is not very well defined. What does it mean to be centered? That question may best be answered by thinking of what being centered *is not.*

You are not centered when:

- You snap.
- You have an immediate big reaction—whether expressed loudly or tightly—to something someone says, does, or fails to do.

- You find yourself pursing your lips, narrowing your eyes, stomping your feet, waving your arms wildly, tightening your fist, banging the table with your hand, flipping someone off, or making other bodily gestures expressing frustration, anger, or intimidation.
- You habitually join alongside others to blame someone else.
- You feel a welling up of negative emotion within you that completely unsettles you, so you shut down, you wall off, you close down.
- You run away, take off, escape into something pleasant or busy, or into a bottle or a pill, or curl up in a ball when something upsets you.
- You routinely come in big, immediately take charge, and start giving orders.
- You routinely withhold, say nothing, remain aloof, disengaged.

Are any of these, or perhaps all, familiar to you? Maybe, maybe not. As a winner, some of the above behaviors might actually work well for you and be in your repertoire, your bag of tricks, your learned habits that you call upon to help make you the winner that you are—to get what you want. But, when you respond out of habit, you are not centered, and you often find yourself regretting your actions and behavior, you tend to burn bridges and alienate others. In more enlightened moments, you may find yourself questioning why you respond that way, or questioning who you are or have become. Your centered self can quickly become subordinate to your personal reactivity.

With an understanding of how being engaged is essential to quality interaction and dialogue, you now see how these behaviors do not fit within the focusing on both self and other concept of transformative conflict theory. But no one is perfect and there is a silver lining to being off center—if you are aware of it when it is happening. That awareness can open up a way for you to be present, attentive, and curious *about yourself*, the inside job that is required and has the potential to shift your outside interaction in a way that is healthy and authentic. You don't have to lose your way, even though it can feel like you are when your center is subordinated to your habitual personal reactivity. Everyone gets stuck from time to time in the habitual ways associated with their personal defense mechanisms. *How might you move more freely and gracefully in relation to others?*

You have had the experience of feeling in harmony with others and within yourself. That is the essence of being centered. It is both within you, in your center, and around you, in how you are with others. Recall how that felt in your body. Remember that feeling. It is a resource.

You have had the experience of feeling in harmony with others and within yourself. That is the essence of being centered.

Being Centered Is Finding and Staying in the Center Within You

When we talk about being centered, you might be thinking, "Here we go; they are going to go off on the whole Zen Buddhist thing." Or you might be thinking, "Yes, exactly, everyone knows you have to attend to your soul, your spirit, your essence, in order to be your highest and best self." Well, yes, but finding the center within you really starts first with your body and your brain. It starts with a

Finding the center within you really starts first with your body and your brain.

very practical look at how our body and mind work together when we are heart centered and how they work when we are not. There are many degrees of centeredness and we may only find the *optimal* state a few times in our lives. Some find it often, others never at all. If you are an athlete, an artist, a surgeon, a performer, you know it as being "in the zone," where you are moving or performing effortlessly, with strength and confidence, and you draw physical, spiritual, and emotional energy from the activity you are engaged in. You act from a place of knowing without thinking, a place of pure intuition—**your heart**. Louise experiences the zone often in her transformative mediation work with others and refers to it as being ***in flow***—when she is aware in the moment, as well as on a meta level, is able to see what is unfolding as if from above, and is still able to surgically intervene at the same time in a way that parts the sea for the clients, out of which emerges for them something unexpected, something intuitive, something said in the perfect meaningful way. It's effortless effort that comes from the heart.

Nothing is quite so identified with the center of your being as your heart. Yes, that organ beating within your chest has a special quality that, for thousands of years, has been associated with aspects of your being that are connected most intimately with who you are as a person—your conscience, your desires, your wisdom, your virtue, your peace, your ***essence***. You feel it within you. It is the place where all these qualities of divine essence reside. It is also identified as the residence of a lot of dark aspects of you too. If you are going to be centered you need to spend time with this place in you and get in touch with its true nature.

Your heart is the conduit for the convertible energy of the body, the movement from off center to being centered. When you are centered, your heart is calm, peaceful, strong, wise, and expansive. You have a good heart. Maybe sometimes you doubt or forget that. But you *do* have a good heart if you are in touch with it and pay attention to it. We believe the true nature of your heart is good. Your heart will tell you when you go off center. Let's talk about how you can get back to center and hold steady there, even when you temporarily lose control, as you inevitably will. Everyone does—it's okay. You live in the real world. Lots of things affect you, throw you off center. That's normal.

Like we said, your heart will tell you when you are not centered. When you are stirred up, when emotions are on overflow, your heart races. When your pulse rate goes up by a mere ten beats per minute, whether two years old or eighty-two, you slip out of gear because the oxygen to your brain is constricted. This applies to you and to the other person you are with. It applies no matter how smart or worldly or experienced you are. So screaming at someone to change their behavior does not work. Indeed, neuroscientists tell us that being screamed at will cause more and longer emotional flooding, and is the last thing the brain will respond to when it is in overflow. In conflict, you have an experience that is mental, emotional, and physical. You become instantly more physically constricted and instantly more emotionally and mentally self-absorbed the moment you experience conflict. The experience of conflict with another person triggers your personal reactivity, hijacking logical thinking because your pre-frontal

In conflict, you have an experience that is mental, emotional, and physical.

brain, where rational thinking occurs, doesn't get the oxygen it needs to work optimally and this happens no matter how saintly or how smart and worldly you are. It doesn't take much for your pre-frontal rational thinking to lose its grip on your consciousness and for more primitive parts of your brain to take over. **It's neuroscience.**[2] Our brain is in three parts, often referred to as the ***Triune Brain***. In conflict, the neural pathways in the brains of women and girls typically change track, engaging the limbic brain, or the emotional brain, which is the center of the brain. For men and boys, the neural pathways in conflict often bypass the limbic brain and flash directly to the brain stem, the reptilian brain, where survival instincts of fight, flight, freeze, and more recently named, feint, are triggered. And, the time it takes for the limbic or reptilian brain to be activated is a mere nanosecond, many times faster than the time it takes for the rational thinking pre-frontal cortex to be engaged. Thus, the likelihood of your brain being hijacked in conflict is high, and your ability to listen deeply and reflect, let alone your ability to be open to another when in a state of conflict, is decreased dramatically. So, suspend your expectations that others will be centered in the face of conflict (and hope that those in your life do the same for you!) because, as a physiological reality, it is very difficult to remain centered when your reactivity is triggered. But you can do it.

The likelihood of your brain being hijacked in conflict is high, and your ability to listen deeply and reflect, let alone your ability to be open to another when in a state of conflict, is decreased dramatically.

Let's look at a scenario.

---

2 See the works of Daniel Goleman, Daniel Siegel.

Imagine you are in the check-out line at the supermarket. You are in a bit of a hurry. Three people behind you in line, the mother of a crying, gooey-nosed two-year-old is yelling wickedly at her child to behave. "Stop It!!" she screams over and over. You are aware that it makes you uncomfortable—you are embarrassed for her, or perhaps you are aware of the judgment rising within you, "What a terrible mother," or "Women should keep their kids at home," or "That poor child is exhausted and this woman insists on bringing her to the grocery store!" Or perhaps you get lost in a memory of when the same thing happened to you and how mortifying it was to be so helpless in a public place. Aware of some of these or other thoughts that race through your head, you take a breath. Fill your whole tank with fresh oxygen, a deep belly breath, and then exhale the energy attached to the thoughts, memories, and triggers. Come back to center, to calm in the face of this storm. Your awareness of what is going on in your mind and in your body is the key starting point. Then, coming from a place of center you might turn to the mother and say, "Some days are hard with kids. Please take my place in line." Being centered helped you to be relational by offering kindness.

Also, consider in your imagination the screaming mother and the crying two-year-old. Indeed, the mother is in as much turmoil as the child. Her screaming at her daughter is because of her emotional flooding, which makes the situation worse for both of them, not to mention adding to the loudness and chaos for you and all the others in that system (the shoppers in the supermarket). Her brain may have lost capacity to think clearly as her oxygen was constricted; she was in the emotional flood zone. With practice, she might have some awareness and know that this is not her normal way of operating. Your response from a place of center provides the pause for her where she might regain some oxygen for herself. And you have contributed to well-being for both of you and the system.

As for the mother, on the spot, she must meet her own strong emotions with a practiced skill of deep listening and reflection. The mother could soothe her emotional reactions by taking deep calming breaths, which would have a calming effect on her daughter as well. She could then consider her options and perhaps remove herself and the screaming two-year-old from the situation by going in the bathroom or outside, even if that meant leaving the cart full of groceries. From a place of center, now with her child and herself out of the stress of the onlookers and the pressure of the line, the mother could get on the same level, eye-to-eye with her two-year-old or sit the child on her lap, hold her, hug her, soothe her—which for a two-year-old is the equivalent of being deeply listened to and reflected. Once the child is calmed, her nose is wiped and she feels loved and understood, then the mother can say, "I know you are upset. Is it okay now? I need to go back into the store and buy our groceries and then we can go home." or "You may hold my hand if you want, and you do not have to ride in the cart, but if you leave my side, I will need to put you back in the cart. I don't want to lose you while I am checking out because I love you, okay?" A two-year-old can hear and understand the why that is offered to explain the behavior. Relational negotiation begins with being centered. Engaged from a place of center creates well-being—relational reciprocity.

Much of being centered comes from the ability to calm the body, namely to calm your primitively instinctual monkey mind and your racing heart. One of the most ancient ways of doing so is by *concentrating on your breath.* Your breath that is with you fifteen to twenty thousand times a day. Your breath that is neutral and has no content. Your breath that is always with you and is constant. Your breath, the first act you took when you entered this world and the last act you will make when you exit. Isn't it exquisite to think of something as simple as the breath in this way? It is the breath that is your personal gateway to allowing yourself to be calm in the face of your storms.

Much of being centered comes from the ability to calm the body, namely to calm your primitively instinctual monkey mind and your racing heart. One of the most ancient ways of doing so is by *concentrating on your breath.*

Being Centered Is Counter-Egoic

When we teach professionals how to engage, negotiate, and respond to difficult situations in relational ways and they experience conflict transformation first hand in their own real conflicts, we regularly hear, "It's amazing, It's so counter-intuitive." It can indeed seem counter-intuitive to our Western culture which values action and displays of power. However, it's not counter-intuitive. Rather, it's completely intuitive. The most accurate and responsive movement you make towards others that you are in conflict with comes from a place of stillness. It is heart centered. That stillness is the quality of being centered, and it is cultivated by breathing deep and awakening your inner-observer. When you are centered, right action will emerge. Being centered is counter to our human defense mechanisms. So, it is more accurate to say that being centered is not counter-intuitive, it is counter-egoic. It is not what our society has spent much time understanding or valuing; we are not taught breathwork for instance in school, particularly in middle and high school where it would be most well placed. And, from a neuroscience perspective, deep breathing is not what your racing brain prompts you to do. In conflict, the brain sends messages to clamp down on the prefrontal oxygen flow believing you are in threat of death. To help the brain function optimally, you need to give it oxygen and the best way to do that is to practice deep breathing. When you practice intentional deep breathing, you also cultivate your heart center. To do these things effectively and in time, effortlessly, you must often *relax your intellect.* Now, *that* is *counter-egoic* and is also certainly counter-cultural!

In any given day, you might have episodes of chaos and moments of getting sucked into a place you didn't anticipate. Whether it's the alarm clock that didn't go off, or the child bellowing two minutes before the bus picks him up for school that he can't find his homework or his shoes. Whether it's the friend in the car pool line who lays a big piece of gossip on you, or the casual lunch conversation in which your colleague complains to you about your mutual boss. Whether it's your good friend complaining about their spouse, who just happens to be your spouse's good friend, or your buddy who works in another division of the corporation and just told you he heard there are going to be more layoffs in your department. In these moments, we have an opportunity to pay attention to our inner selves before doing anything.

Being centered is paying attention to your heart, mind, and your body. To pay attention, you will need oxygen. If your mind is jumbled, it means breathing through your thoughts before you say or do anything. If your body is unsettled, it means bringing some awareness and acceptance of this state, not fighting it. Fighting your chaotic insides puts a clamp on the emotional turmoil that has energy and wants to be expressed. You might say, "Controlling my emotions is a good thing." Indeed, this may sound appealing, but it is actually quite destructive and dangerous, and those who do this often generally suffer the consequences including ulcers, high blood pressure, obesity, digestive complaints, and hypertension, not to mention skin ailments and other manifestations of persistent stress.

Fighting back the chaos and clamping it down buries that strong emotional energy internally. That energy needs an outlet; your organs, belly, and heart are often the repositories, and the more you ignore or clamp down, the more destructive the energy is on your body, and often later on other people. Instead, if you honor and befriend the emotional unbalance in the moment by giving it room through your breath, you are likely to find its energy released when you exhale. In that moment, you have a much better chance to regain your authentic center again. It's there; it's waiting for you always. Your breath will lead you there.

If you honor and befriend the emotional unbalance in the moment by giving it room through your breath, you are likely to find its energy released when you exhale.

Being Centered Is Finding and Staying Centered Among Others—Being Alert to Triangling

In addition to finding the center within yourself, being centered calls you to find and stay centered in your relationship to others.

Losing your centeredness in relationship to others typically happens when someone comes to you with a complaint, gripe, or piece of gossip about someone else. So, when your colleague tells you on Friday that your boss, Mr. Uptight, wants all the projections for the next year's budget by Monday, breathe. Take a deep breath and find your center before you respond. This will probably mean deep listening, offering a reflection, and not responding right away.

When caught off-guard, if you respond right away, you are probably not coming from a place of centeredness. You could get sucked down the rabbit hole into your neighbor or your colleague's complaining. It is easy to fall. All it takes is for you to agree with them or respond by saying nothing, which in our Western society often is translated into agreement. There is a moment of discernment, but it is likely that, without being centered, you bypass it and habitually take a familiar path of agreeing with or saying nothing, thus escalating conflict and division.

Out of habit or in a reactive moment you might respond, "Oh my God, that jerk!" or "Oh, great (sarcastically). There goes my weekend." Without even thinking, you respond by agreeing. It's fuel for what we call off-centered triangling. Triangling[3] is when you become part of someone else's conflict without even realizing it, because you are not aware, you are not in tune with your inner cues, and you respond out of anger or fear or helplessness or just laziness. You are not being centered; *you join with another person in a triangle in opposition to a third person who is not present.* Triangling

> Triangling is when you become part of someone else's conflict without even realizing it.

3 See e.g., the work of Virginia Satir or *Interpersonal Conflict* by William Wilmot.

is a strategy you may have learned on the playground as a child, generally perfected by most little girls by the time they reach fifth grade. Or, you may have seen it in your home of origin thousands of times. *It is an unhealthy way to build coalitions, generally in order to gain power.* You gain power and become closer to someone by being with them in opposition to a third person. If you think of it for a moment, this is a strategy you know well. It is often used by winners to gain power, saying, "The enemy of my enemy is my friend." History is full of examples of triangling on a large and often dangerous scale, think Nazis, aligned with German people, in opposition to Jews, or Jihadists, aligned with Muslims, in opposition to American "Infidels" or, to be balanced about it, Neoconservatives, aligned with American people, in opposition to Islamic "Terrorists." Or how about purely American examples—Democrats, aligned with working class Americans, in opposition to "Right-Wing Conservative Extremists" or Republicans, aligned with freedom loving Americans, in opposition to "Left-Wing Radical Liberals." It is just about the most toxic way of being in relationship with others, causing untold amounts of violence, suffering, death, and destruction.

Triangling: You gain power and become closer to someone by being with them in opposition to a third person.

Triangling, as we said, is used to build coalitions. Your response in joining a coalition against someone builds momentum for the coalition building effort. Let's look again at that more personalized, closer-to-home example. It is grist for the rumor mill when your colleague goes to the next person in the office or corporation with the same complaint about the boss and tells them, "Yeah, when I told Pete about what the boss did, you should have seen his face. He's pissed too." Before you know it, a coalition against someone else is created and you are swept up in it, whether, in hindsight, you want to be or not.

There are often consequences to this that are neither desirable for the coalition builders nor for the joiners. As the coalition builds, the demonization of the third person gets exaggerated and distorted in order to draw in as many people as possible, even if they are objectively reasonable and neutral. The outcome of the coalition building is often an extreme characterization of the other —a characterization that is false, especially as broadly applied to a large group of people commonly labeled. Even where there may have been a kernel of truth, the triangle distorts and credibility is sacrificed in the end. Even when there may be genuine, even celebrated, differences, the triangling process exaggerates the differences, loses sight of the commonalities and injects greater friction into relationships.

Furthermore, as your experience will tell you, once you are **in** a triangle, it can be very hard to get **out** and reclaim a non-aligned posture. If you back out of a triangle you can be accused of sympathizing with or even supporting the demonized other. You risk alienating and breaking your relationship with the person who came to you with the complaint. You risk being ostracized yourself from the coalition group and being branded a traitor. Coalitions built in this way imprison with fear those who join them and prevent any authentic shifts in understanding of the demonized other.

Triangling is especially a trap if you are agreeable, if you consider yourself peaceful or non-confrontational or conflict avoidant, because, when you are approached by someone who has an *issue* with a third person, the tendency is to nod or to agree and go along with what was said by the other person. But even if you follow the sage advice to stay out of it—not getting involved and not saying anything—this can have the same negative consequences as if you had agreed. In this hyper-connected, crowded world we live in, saying nothing and doing nothing is often construed as agreement and consent, and before you know it, you get lumped into the coalition: *the entire department* is upset.

> Triangling is especially a trap if you are agreeable, if you consider yourself peaceful or non-confrontational or conflict avoidant, because, when you are approached by someone who has an *issue* with a third person, the tendency is to nod or to agree and go along with what was said by the other person.

Worse yet, when you are responding from a place that is off center and you have a tendency to agree because it's easy or it makes you feel cozy with and in the same situation with another person, or even safe momentarily, then there is a dangerous tendency actually *to add to* the problem. First, that cozy feeling you give to them, harmlessly forming a flimsy alliance, may prevent you from later being able to state your own views or from finding out more about the situation or from exploring other options for action. Also, as if agreeing with and forming false or flimsy alliances is not bad enough, you could even add to the brushfire of others' complaints and gossip with your own gasoline by making additional comments about your boss such as, "I believe it. I remember he did this to us last year too." The complainers disseminate complaints and gossip, which spreads like fire and you are caught up in it.

When that happens, *camps* begin to form in the office. This can happen too in families, or in communities about decisions made in local government. It can happen with any group, whether it's a group of three people or of millions. You know what this looks like as it is quite common and destructive to working relationships. Certain people who feel cozy with each other alienate themselves from other people who are doing the same kind of triangling amongst themselves. They all become disconnected from each other and often the original problem: the *real* concern held by the vast majority of people in the group—that there is not enough notice and time to do a good job for the boss (when he asked on Friday for the projections on Monday)—goes unattended, unaddressed. In its place is created an additional problem: the malcontent of gossip and the politics of destructive coalitions. Triangling is part of the landscape of our day-to-day existence, especially for winners. Doing nothing or adding to triangles is not being relational.

Being Centered Is Choosing Not to Triangle in Your Families and Family Systems

Make no mistake, triangling isn't just a political, community, workplace, or extended family phenomenon. A triangling scenario might also easily exist right in your own home. Like when your middle school-aged son tattles on his teenage sister that she was still texting or on Facebook way past midnight, and you agree with your middle-schooler how wrong it is and you might even add to the problem by saying, "Let's hope *you* aren't like that when you get older." Whoa! A triangling response that doesn't come from a place of center not only creates distance between family members and causes a sense of separateness from each other, it can create an additional fracture in the relationship between the other person and you. The *real* original concern that the younger child had when coming to you may have included such tender things as being worried about his older sister, not wanting his older sister to get bad grades, hearing her crying because something mean was put on Facebook, seeking love and attention for himself, being confused about parenting standards. However, because the parent responded in a way that was not centered, the real original concern that the child had never gets addressed. And, for those interested in family systems and how the decisions and responses of two people affect the whole, consider that middle-schooler. Is he now closer and more connected to his sister? Probably not, indeed the parent created a new wedge between them: I will love you more because you are not like she is. What will happen to the middle-schooler when he is a teenager and is on Facebook at midnight? Will he be more likely to be deceitful and even feel shame because the parent's response never dealt with the behavior, but made it about the child herself?

> Triangling in your family relations unintentionally causes great harm.

Triangling in your family relations unintentionally causes great harm. Likewise, when the leaders of businesses, departments, teams, boards of directors, non-profits, government agencies, and churches complain about or demonize others inside the "family" that they manage or live with, and the response pattern of triangling is repeated over and over, it causes the kind of emotional wounding and false alliances that take years for businesses to change or months of outside intervention in conflict transformation to shift, and often take decades for communities to recover from.

So, when your colleague comes to you complaining about the boss, remember, this person is coming to you. They obviously like you or respect you or know you exist, at the very least. They are looking for an ear. The fact that you work in the same business has significance. You have a relationship with them. Each community, from the nuclear family to the multinational corporation and the community of nations, is its own system, a family system, with inter-working and inter-dependent people, all inter-related. The flash fire of triangling causes great damage. The fires of responses that are off center and do not come from the heart center burn through a family system. Next time you are faced with a triangling situation, consider not aligning with or adding to the problem by staying centered. We will address what a centered and unitive response can look like, but first, we want to share with you another type of triangling that is equally damaging to systems.

There is also danger in triangling even if you **don't** align and agree with the person coming to you with a complaint. Let's say that, instead of agreeing with and even adding to, you might be inclined to dismiss the complaint or to dismiss your colleague personally. You might say to yourself, *This is just a bunch of nonsense and I'm having nothing to do with it.* And you might tell your colleague just that. Maybe you say, "You complaining again? Be glad you have a job."

Or perhaps you might fashion a more benign or tempered response, "Well, somebody will figure it all out" or "Yeah, well, I'm just happy to be working." Whew! You might think to yourself, "I got myself out of that one." But we all know you didn't. Why? Because a person who has a problem or a beef with someone else and comes to *you* about the problem they have with that person is looking for a number of things. If they are off center and unbalanced, they are likely to be seeking alignment, and when they don't get it, and instead get from you an experience of being dismissed or put down, then, in their own unsettledness, they are likely to seek out others in the family system, such as other neighbors, colleagues, co-workers, or family members. Their response now is likely to have more energy and to include *you* as well and sound like, "You got the memo about the due date on the projections for the budget? Stinks doesn't it? You know what Bill said? Says it's no big deal. What a suck-up!" What is the result? A new set of triangles. New problems, and now fractures in relationships you didn't have before—against *you*—new cliques. And you were trying not to get involved!

There might also be some who secretly agree with you, and so that alliance is formed as well, silently. The system also becomes predictable over time with which groups will respond in which way to new requests or demands. The system loses responsiveness. The system becomes non-dynamic. Ruts develop. Systems become closed, stuck in dysfunctional, predictable, non-flexible patterns. Over time, with repeated triangling responses, divisions emerge where there were none, and you may have contributed to this in the *way* you responded—off center, out of balance.

Being Centered Is Being Complaint Free

Triangling is serious business, so let's talk about how to be centered when encountering potentially destructive triangling. In devoting a life to understanding conflict in organizations and in families, we believe there is a *unitive, restorative* way to handle

> We believe there is a *unitive, restorative* way to handle situations where triangling might occur. It starts with you and how you deal with things that cause you grief, pain, and discontent.

situations where triangling might occur. It starts with you and how you deal with things that cause you grief, pain, and discontent. It may seem obvious, but the best way to be centered and prevent destructive triangling is to *avoid being the one who* ***starts*** *the triangling phenomenon by complaining to another person and expecting alignment.* You strive to be complaint free.[4]

So what does that mean? Sure, you have opinions and hurts and things you do not like. It takes awareness and discipline not to grouse, gossip, put others down, or speak poorly of someone else behind their back. Striving to be complaint free means that you are relational in response to things that trigger a negative reaction within you—things that piss you off, annoy you, push your buttons. As discussed above, when this happens, you do your best to stay internally centered. Also, as we discuss ahead, you remain grounded in truth, focusing on what *is,* not what should be or could be. You focus on the reality of the situation. You call upon your internal well of kindness, generosity, and humility. Then, *you make the decision not to carry your negative reaction and express it to another person, unless that person is the one who can effect the change you desire, and your request for change has objective legitimacy.* You choose not to complain to a third person about someone else. You choose not to lure another person to triangle with you in opposition to the person or entity you have a beef or problem with.

4 See Bowen, Will, *A Complaint Free World (2007, 2013).*

Does this mean you just have to put up with something that is bothering you? Grin and bear it? Shut up and just do your job? Well, as we like to say in the mediation room, maybe and maybe not! Being complaint free does not mean you are a victim or that you passively suffer injustices, ill treatment, and abuse. It also does not mean you do not express your concerns or viewpoints. However, it also does not mean that you seek to control the behavior of others by pointing out all of the ways in which their behavior does not meet your standards of propriety. So there is a healthy way to remain centered while also seeking to address concerns and problems. It looks like this:

First: Is what is bothering you something that you, or anybody else for that matter, have little or no power to change? If so, then you don't bother complaining about it. Even if it's just a complaint about the weather and you're just making small talk, why put forth that negative vibe? You might think it will help break the ice with someone and start a friendly conversation, but you just don't do it. Instead you break the ice with a positive comment.

And when there are big issues that may seem totally out of your control to address, when you really can't go to anyone directly to address the problem—like your unhappiness with tax policies or decisions to use military force—you engage others in discussion and debate, and you take a relational problem-solving approach. It's not complaining to discuss your views with others on big issues. In fact, if you are silent about big problems just because you feel they are issues that are over your head and out of your control, you might actually be complicit in condoning them. You are a citizen, a member of the community, and what you think matters. When you are relational, you do express your views, but you don't complain. You don't point blame at a person or group thus setting up, joining, or adding to a destructive triangle. You address issues and policies, and resist attacks on people and their personalities. Building coalitions to address wrongs, injustices, and problems is not complaining and destructive triangling when it involves dialogue on issues. We encourage that. But when your complaint becomes an attack on another person or group of people, dialogue on issues is lost and the goal is merely to demonize the opposing group. So, you don't just express the negative side of your views and stop there. It's not "I don't like . . ." Instead it's "I would like . . ." You look for solutions. And you engage in dialogue, asking others what their views are, in an attitude of deep listening. You work to get information and to become more knowledgeable about the consequences associated with the change you seek. You seek to persuade and influence others, and you listen and are open to being persuaded and influenced by them.

Building coalitions to address wrongs, injustices, and problems is not complaining and destructive triangling when it involves dialogue on issues. We encourage that.

Second: If the problem is one that is not too big, is there something you can do differently to change the situation? Often you can head off a complaint at the pass and save yourself needless suffering by changing your own behavior.

You look at that option first. This doesn't mean that you just put up with something you don't like, or that you go way out of your way to avoid dealing with the issue or the person, you simply consider, "Is there something not too burdensome I can do that will make the situation better for myself?" If there is, then you do it and make the complaint disappear. There are a myriad of possibilities for constructive simple action.

Third: Is the problem one that is objectively real or is it a result of your unreasonable expectations or your inability to deal with things as they *are* as opposed to how you think they *should* be? This calls upon you to be grounded, which is discussed ahead more fully, but if your complaint stems from your egoic need to control others, to always be right, and to always know best, then your request for change probably is not objectively legitimate. This doesn't mean that you ignore bad behavior, but you don't let your pride, arrogance and ego get in the way of being open to the ways of others. You engage with them before criticizing and complaining. You are humble in considering that your way might not be the only way. You are generous in not picking apart and correcting every little imperfection in another person—especially in your family, where being relational begins.

Fourth: If the problem is one that someone else can address, then you take the issue to that person directly. If you have a problem with a particular person, you go to that person only. When you go to them, you are clear, stating the facts surrounding the issue as you know them. You do not

> exaggerate or generalize. You do not minimize or gloss over. You know that underlying your complaint there is a request for something. You make a request for the change that you desire. You may need to negotiate with them, and you do that relationally, using all of the tools and disciplines associated with being relational, which you will learn throughout this book.

Following this path, you avoid becoming the person who *starts* a wave of destructive triangling. You can also be the person who *stops* destructive triangling by offering a unitive response. Let's look at how to do that.

Being Centered Is Choosing Unitive Triangling

Say you are aware of the feeling that you are about to get sucked into someone else's problem or conflict, it might be a flutter of your heart, or a quickening of your pulse, or maybe it's a certain excitement or even shock at the gossip that is shared with you. Now what? You remain calm and aware of the unsteadiness or the flutter in you. Your body provides wonderful cues that something important is happening in the exchange, in the interaction you are now in, whether you invited it or not.

Now you pause and listen deeply and fully, not yet responding. You find the center within you through your breath. Pause and breathe. Feel that belly breath. No one else will even notice. It's all personal, just for you. Let the oxygen fill your body. Listen fully and completely to the complaint, the gripe, the gossip, the putdown. Suspend your judgment so you can listen fully without having to judge. You are aware of the leaning you may have one way or the other to join or to dismiss. You remind yourself of possible destructive triangling responses—agreeing with and adding to the complaint, or dismissing the complaint and putting down the complainer. Instead, you honor the speaker's situation and honor your own presence. The other person complaining may be loud or ugly or funny. They may make you uncomfortable. Don't fight that, instead befriend that, be curious about it and stay steady. Stay centered, fully awake, and open—ready to be responsive.

When the person stops complaining about the other person, *offer a reflection*—part of being engaged. Reflect back exactly what they said. This is not reflecting back what you think they meant to say. This is *reflecting back exactly what they said, their words, not yours*—their stated meaning, not your interpretation. Wait, pause and breathe again. Repeat as necessary. Be amazed at the effect your centeredness has on them. They are likely to calm down and soften the rough edges of their complaint as they sense that you are not immediately joining in it. They are also likely to expand on the complaint and get underneath to a core concern that is often rooted in fear. What a service you just provided, making a choice to live relationally by staying centered and not getting sucked in or adding to a problem, which often in turn provides them the space and opportunity to become more open to themselves and their otherwise narrow experience. Being centered allows you to be responsive, not reactive. Being centered allows them to think more clearly, more thoughtfully, more fully about a situation as well.

> Being centered allows you to be responsive, not reactive.

Responses to others that are not centered come from your own discomfort, inadequacies, fear, past hurts, and anger which are all forms of ***personal reactivity***. Reactivity rather than thoughtful responsiveness is fuel for triangling where you become part of someone else's conflict without even realizing it. There is an aspect of forbearance in being centered. Whether it is in the moment that you pause rather than operating out of personal reactivity or it is in the much more disciplined act of holding your sharp tongue or keeping your prattling to yourself, there is a decision to be your own best self, a decision that emanates from being centered.

You can do a lot when engaging from a place of center, depending on the situation. It allows you to be able to listen deeply, even if for a mere two or three minutes. When you offer a reflection of the real essence of what they said, it allows them to feel a connection with themselves, to hear themselves, sometimes as if for the first time. It also allows the other person to feel the connection with you. The interaction becomes more personalized. Coming from center allows an opening, a space, where the speaker, complaining and unhappy, now has *a place to unload and be restored* to their own center where they can consider alternatives. In that space, the speaker is now safe and has nothing to resist or defend against. In that space, they might even edit or retract some of what they said about the person they were complaining about. They may have a moment of insight or clarity—that they had exaggerated a bit, their view of the person they have a problem with is too narrow, or maybe they embellished or puffed it up and it's really not quite that way. They may even chuckle at themselves. All this transformation has the potential to occur because you engaged from a place of center.

In this changed atmosphere, now, depending on your relationship to the person—as colleague, boss, family member, or fellow citizen—you can offer things like, "I understand part of your concern, but I also have questions as to why you think that." Or "I see your point of view and appreciate it. I would like to know more of the total story from the others, and then see from there what might be done." Or "Yes, I have found that person or situation to be difficult too; but I've also known that person to be fair or willing to discuss an issue. You might want to consider meeting with her about it." Or "I understand that you are upset about this. Are you thinking of doing anything about it? Maybe or maybe not? Can I help you think it through?" These questions open doors for the other to consider options and think about information that is needed for informed decision-making and action that promotes well-being. There is a steadiness in being relational, and because you are approaching a situation engaging from your heart, you respond more authentically. You ask the kind of questions that others might not dare to ask, not because you are brazen or naïve, but because you are engaged and responding with a curiosity and a desire for fully informed thinking and robust understanding. This allows you to work hard to get information and to be willing to give information.

> Coming from a place of center does not guide or direct conversation in one way, nor does it seek to control negotiations. Being centered allows you to follow and to experience the natural rhythm of a conversation or a negotiation.

You are not fearful about the response that you might get to an open question—a question to which you do not know the answer, a question that is not leading or answerable with a yes or no. Coming from a place of center does not guide or direct conversation in one way, nor does it seek to control negotiations. Being centered allows you to follow and to experience the natural rhythm of a conversation or a negotiation. They are not linear. It's not a step-by-step thing—identify the problem, explore interests, brainstorm solutions, form agreement. No. You have the ability to follow a meandering and sometimes circular path. And you follow that path through to quality decision making, which is not always about problem solving in that moment. You refrain from trying to force others to do what you think is best because you engage from a place of deeper knowing and belief that together, through dialogue, clarity will emerge and a well-informed decision will be made. Action, then or later, is then a natural byproduct.

You believe that there is something positive that can come out of the interaction itself, and you set a positive frame, making this belief transparent. You know from Transformative Conflict Theory and the theory of relational reciprocity that something positive often does come out of quality interactions. Your belief is also supported by neuroscience, which confirms that the brain scans for the positive frame, and upon hearing it or experiencing it, becomes more alert and receptive. So, you begin your interactions with, "I am glad we are talking about this and hope and believe something positive will result." You are patient, not hurried. You have confidence in whatever unfolds.

Consider your own life, those times when you responded in a thoughtful and centered way, without personal reactivity, even though you may have been like a tornado or a fire on the inside. You centered yourself, took some deep breaths in the moment or over a period of time. You regrouped and responded differently than you otherwise would have. When you choose to respond to the triangles of daily living in ways that come from a place of center, you create a *unitive triangle*—a way of relating to the others involved that restores the quality of the interaction itself, a way that fosters personal strength and openness to the other person as a first option. Your choice of unitive triangling rather than destructive triangling not only helps to restore the fractured interaction between two people or groups, but also enhances the quality of interaction between you and the complainer, and additionally strengthens the experience between you and the third person complained about when and if they learn of your tempered and steady response.

> *Unitive triangle*—
> a way of relating to the others involved that restores the quality of the interaction itself, a way that fosters personal strength and openness to the other person as a first option.

When you engage from a place of center, this is another huge payoff for you. As you practice being centered and responding to triangles in a unitive way, expect restoration of your own personal strength and a more steady sense of yourself when confronted with future conflicted situations. Anticipate the benefit of a new or renewed openness to different points of view with the strength to explore collaborative solutions with others in ways you never before realized. When faced with triangling situations, which are everywhere, you remain centered and you choose unitive triangling as a first option, which increases

> When faced with triangling situations, you remain centered and you choose unitive triangling as a first option, which increases well-being for all, including yourself.

well-being for all, including yourself. That is a powerful way to create change without destruction and division.

And if you are a parent of young children, you have scores of opportunities to foster unitive triangling each time a child complains to you about a sibling, especially in those situations where the sibling in question is also present, including common scenarios such as boys roughhousing too aggressively and the younger grouses or squeals about being hurt or picked on. Rather than jumping in to align with one or the other, to dismiss or correct the child you are displeased with, instead consider a reflection and assist the complaining child to make a request of the other child. You will be amazed at what happens.

Questions for Your Consideration

In exploring Being Centered consider the following questions. If you are not sure about your answers, go back and visit the chapter.

- What do you notice is going on in your body when you are in conflict?
- In a difficult or uncomfortable situation, which of your responses to the situation makes things worse?
- Thinking of a difficult or bad experience you had with someone, how could your response to them have been different?
- How do you relax your personal reactivity when someone says something to you that you think is completely false or outrageous?

- What do you do when you have a complaint about someone?
- What do you do when someone comes to you with a complaint about another person?
- What do you do to try to prevent unhealthy coalitions from forming when people disagree?

Chapter 5

Being Grounded

While being engaged and being centered largely have to do with how you act, how you present yourself to others, and how you respond to them, being grounded is different. It has to do with your thinking, the way you experience what is going on around you and what you think about it. Your thinking will affect how you are able to engage with others, or not. Your thinking will affect how you are able to remain centered, or not. A lack of groundedness can completely undermine your best efforts to be relational because your expectations for yourself and others are out of line with reality.

You may be caught up in thoughts that create much of your suffering and your frustration with your life and the people in it, thoughts that are essentially untrue, thoughts that are not grounded in truth, thoughts that become beliefs which limit your ability to see your world as it truly is. This negatively affects you and others, gets in the way of positive relationships, and often needlessly escalates conflict.

You will know that your thoughts are in fact delusions, disconnected from truth, when:

- You think some situation, some thing, or someone, including yourself, will *never* change or will *always* be a certain way.
- You give up and passively become a victim to your circumstances.
- You are mired in thinking about what you deserve, what should be, what ought to be or could be, if only . . .
- You are lost in dreaming about a wonderful future without doing anything to create it.
- You are stuck in the past and how good it was compared to now.
- You obsess about the past and what could have been, should have been, or ought to have been, if only . . .
- You judge a person or situation on a mere snippet of information—a blink.
- You apply labels to individuals, groups, and organizations and believe them.
- You act habitually based on your coping strategies and without self-awareness.

On the other hand, when you are grounded, you have the sense that *you are in touch with things as they are.* You are grounded in reality. In addition to the mental aspect, there is a physical sense to it. You feel the earth beneath you. You shift your attention literally to your feet. You feel the floor of the car with your left foot, or the rug or the pavement beneath your feet,

When you are grounded, you have the sense that *you are in touch with things as they are.* You are grounded in reality.

wherever you are—even the sand or the forest floor. Or you use your imagination to feel the solid ground beneath you. Using the focus of your mind to re-ground your thinking brings you back to feeling solid. You have a sensation of support and well-being and indeed you are in that moment well supported by the ground beneath you. You are full of awareness, without anticipation, analysis, or evaluation. You are joyful, at ease. Let's look at the mental discipline that can help you find this state.

Being Grounded Is Embracing the "Maybe, Maybe Not"—Being Open

One of our favorite expressions in our mediation practice is "maybe, maybe not." We use it to help convey the idea that situations faced, options considered, and judgments made are rarely absolute and fixed. In mediation, participants often are making judgments about themselves and others, and about their options, motivations, and so on. The concept of ***maybe, maybe not*** helps them see that other realities are possible if they can relax their attachment to the one that they have seized upon. This helps them remain open and can do the same for you. When a statement is made by another person or when you feel the urge to make a statement assessing a situation or passing judgment, you can give yourself space and time to consider alternatives by thinking to yourself or possibly saying out loud to another person, "Maybe, maybe not." By doing so you remain open to other possibilities, other views,

"Maybe, maybe not," conveys the idea that situations faced, options considered, and judgments made are rarely absolute and fixed.

other judgments. You do not commit to a particular version of the truth. You do not align with another in a possible destructive triangle, nor do you set yourself in opposition to them.

The ***maybe, maybe not*** concept, when you use it with others from a place of center, also lets them know that you respect their ability to decide for themselves and make their own judgments. So when giving advice to another person or presenting them with an option, you give them your input and opinion, but you don't substitute your judgment for theirs, you don't override their judgment with yours. In this way you are a better sounding board for others. You are a better listener. You are relational. You might say to a friend who is considering an important decision, such as moving to a new town, "So you are thinking about moving? Maybe? Maybe not?" This preserves their sense of self-determination and helps them own the decision that they make. It helps them with their discernment of a path rather than feeling like a path was chosen for them. It invites them to look closer at the situation. It's not demanding them to, "Look closer at that." It is saying, you **might** want to look closer at that—maybe, maybe not." You are not attached to the idea of guiding them to a particular decision, instead you are fully committed to quality interaction and dialogue and informed decision-making. It is supportive and encourages active discernment, slowing down the rash judgment and decision process, which makes for better, more reasoned judgments as compared with judgments made out of personal reactivity which are, as we have discussed, not made from a place of being centered.

Being grounded means you acknowledge for yourself and for others that you might *not know* what is, **in fact**, true or best. If you state a viewpoint, it can be strong, yet still open to inquiry. If you make a statement and the response is "That's not true!" you pause and you are rigorous about truth. That means that you acknowledge that what you **think** could lead you to conclusions that might **not** in fact be true. You are open to the possibility that your analysis may be flawed, based on too little information, or unduly influenced by past experiences, by others' influence, or by cultural biases. So, instead of jumping to conclusions, instead of making a "blink" judgment, instead of assuming you know something, you choose to **suspend judgment** for a period of time.

Being grounded means you acknowledge for yourself and for others that you might *not know* what is, **in fact**, true or best.

You embrace the idea that there are other possibilities and that the version of the truth that seems most likely to you *may* be true, but maybe *not*. This leads you to interact with others in a different way. You are engaged. You remain curious. You seek information. You use your creativity and imagination to help you consider different versions of truth that might be possible. When you do this with others it is an act of generosity on your part, but it will also pay great dividends back to you because you will avoid a great deal of suffering and conflict that is fueled by your flawed judgments.

Embracing the ***maybe, maybe not*** will help you avoid needless suffering. Why do we say that? Ask yourself, "What does my suffering look like?" It is you *arguing with reality*. You become agitated, you are not centered, when you look at the people in your life, the situations in your life, the cards that you are dealt, and say that they *should be different* than they are. Or you might say that they *could* be different and better if only . . . Or that they *would* be different and better, if only . . . You also create suffering for others by imposing upon them your view of how they should or should not be, what they should or should not do. That doesn't mean you have an *anything goes* mentality, as we discuss below with regard to healthy boundaries, but it does mean that you let go of the shoulda, coulda, woulda thinking you have that separates you from finding joy and contentment in what *is*—the way things **are**, the way people are—not how they would, could, or should be. You are more open.

When you change your thinking in this simple but powerful way, you can be centered and engaged with any situation. But you may find this very hard to do, because, without realizing it, you may be very attached to your thinking. Some of your thoughts that cause you the most suffering may have become strongly held beliefs. You may have very deeply grooved habits of mind.

Much has been written in philosophy, theology, psychology, and self-help literature about the problems associated with becoming attached to thoughts that argue with reality.[5] You have beliefs and thoughts that you have attached to, you identify with, and you have come to hold as *truth* in your heart and mind. Sometimes they are very simple like, "fish gotta swim and birds gotta fly," or more complex like "kids need a father and a mother." Or really complex like "Jesus is the Son of God," or "people should be kind." Being grounded doesn't mean you give up everything you believe in, but it does mean that you care a lot about not getting attached to thoughts and beliefs that you do not *know* are true,

5 See e.g., Katie, Byron, *Loving What Is* (2002).

particularly if your attachment to the belief causes you suffering because it is contrary to reality or if your belief imposes suffering on others because it is not believed by them. You show you care by being attentive to your thoughts and how they affect you and others around you.

Being grounded doesn't mean you give up everything you believe in, but it does mean that you care a lot about not getting attached to thoughts and beliefs that you do not *know* are true, particularly if your attachment to the belief causes you suffering because it is contrary to reality or if your belief imposes suffering on others because it is not believed by them.

Being attentive to your thoughts literally means observing them rather than being ruled by them. You are not trying to control your mind so as to totally block out your thoughts. Thoughts happen! You have a brain and it thinks. So you notice your thoughts as they appear and disappear, as they shift and change. They are like clouds in the sky or waves breaking on the shore. They appear. They pass. You let them pass. You make internal space for the energy associated with those thoughts to flow around barriers so they do not get blocked and backed up in your consciousness.

Being attentive to your thoughts literally means observing them rather than being ruled by them.

Some thoughts will come back to you over and over again because they are interesting to you or because something or someone in your life stimulates you to think them. The thoughts may be positive and joyful. The thoughts may be negative or troubling. The thoughts may be evil or dark. You pay attention to that, but you don't resist it, you don't get lost in it, and most importantly you do not attach to the thoughts in an unhealthy way. The thoughts are not you. You are much more than your thoughts. With thoughts about positive experiences, fantasies, and desires, you do not become so attached to them that you develop a craving for more of them and more of the things that created them. That kind of attachment leads to disconnectedness from others. You know the craving can become an addiction—obsessive thinking about something you become very wrapped up in. With negative thoughts, you do not harbor them in a way that grows resentment and fear like a cancer within you. You know that fear and resentment can manifest themselves in illness, anger, and even violence.

So you observe your thoughts, and when you feel your thoughts adversely affecting your ability to be centered, when you notice yourself stuck on a thought, you shift your attention to being grounded, finding your feet on the ground, and you remember the idea of ***maybe, maybe not*** and ask yourself, *Is that thought really true? Do I know that it is true? Is there another possible reality or way of looking at the person or situation that I am not seeing?* You choose to look at it harder. Like Rafiki invites in *The Lion King*, "**Look harder**, Simba. You see?" And what you see when you look harder is the reality that what you think is maybe true, but maybe not. Knowing this, you are willing to make room for other possibilities, reality as it is—good, bad, ugly, disappointing, sweet, tender, or joyful.

It takes practice and a change in your mind-set and, perhaps even your entire worldview, but you are committed to being grounded, and one of the beliefs that you are now open and receptive to is the belief that being grounded can help bring you greater contentment and an enhanced ability to collaborate with others and create positive outcomes. With this belief in mind, let's take the invitation to 'look harder' at some of the types of thinking that get in the way of being grounded, the type of thinking you might be attached to that can lead to your suffering and suffering for others you interact with.

Being Grounded Is Letting Go of Always and Never

Another side of the ***maybe, maybe not*** coin, is the idea that, in being grounded, in considering whether what you think is in fact true or not, you *let go of absolutes* like ***always*** and ***never***. You know that when you say to someone, "You always . . ." or "You never . . . ," that you are goading them into an escalation of conflict. Why? Because the statement you make is false and it triggers a reaction on the part of the other person to defend and perhaps fire back at you their own always or never statement—thus engaging in the energetic reciprocity of conflict. It is unproductive in conversation with another person, and it is equally unproductive in the conversation you have with yourself in your thinking.

When you are grounded, you *expect change*, even those changes that might not be welcomed. You have a stance, a rootedness, that can accept change because you know that nothing is permanent, everything is transitory. The words Catholics hear when receiving ashes on their foreheads on Ash Wednesday come to mind,

When you are grounded, you *expect change*, even those changes that might not be welcomed. You have a stance, a rootedness, that can accept change because you know that nothing is permanent, everything is transitory.

"Remember you are dust and to dust you shall return." You know that there are a multitude of simultaneously interacting factors in your world and your life that guarantee only one thing, that everything will change and will not be as it is at this moment. With many of the circumstances swirling around you, you remind yourself, *This too shall pass.* It does not mean you avoid reality. Just the opposite, you engage with reality tempered by knowing it is temporal and each moment, each interaction, is just one moment in the grand context. But, consider all the times when you get spun up in a situation as if it is absolute, as if it will never change or go away. Notice how quick you are to move into never or always thinking. Particularly when the situation brings you pain, triggers frustration, or incites anger.

Here is an example. As a winner, you might be an employer with people working under your supervision. Something goes wrong at work and you think, *That employee has screwed up again! She just doesn't get it. She'll never improve. I'm going to fire her.* A grounded way to approach that thought, as we discussed, is to suspend judgment and look harder. You think, *Hold on. Maybe she could improve, maybe not? Maybe it's best to let her go, maybe not?* Remember, when you are grounded, the energy in your frustration or anger or despair has a place to flow around barriers rather than get trapped. You think, *Okay, so I want to fire her . . . What would happen if I fired her? What would be necessary to fire her? What would I do to replace her? What might she do when I fire her? Does she do anything valuable so that I would not want to fire her? Can she be trained? Can her duties be shifted around so she can succeed? Is there something I can change about how I manage her?* There are many more questions you might ask. This is much more active discernment. It is not procrastination or avoidance. It has intention.

Your act of engaging in that discernment comes from your commitment to being grounded and open. You are centered, so you don't complain to others and you decide to take your concerns directly to the employee for an open and honest discussion. As we discuss in later chapters, that is an act of generosity, kindness, and humility. You give of your time, your intellectual and emotional energy, and your patience. You set aside your pride and ego to be engaged with her, believing in the capacity that you and she have together to move through conflict with quality interactions and dialogue, even over uncomfortable topics. You do this because you are relational and it is good for her, good for you. It's just plain good, even if the outcome is painful and difficult and you decide it is best for her to find other employment. You may part ways, but you do so with integrity.

Being grounded works in the other direction of interaction as well. Take the situation of an employee who is miserable, hates her boss, hates her job, feels stuck, and sucks it up until she cannot take it anymore. She walks out one day saying she quits. Had she decided instead to stay grounded and engage her boss, she may have found in their face-to-face meeting that the boss had no idea how miserable she was, that the boss finds her valuable and that there are other tasks or jobs for her had she asked. Or, perhaps the other tasks or jobs are not available, and so they discuss her resignation. They find that she has no other job lined up and the boss offers her the chance to stay until she finds new employment so long as she gives the boss two weeks notice, helps to train a new person, only spends lunch hours and breaks in the job search and does not triangle with other employees. They re-established their connection, she lets go of her attachment to "I hate my job and my boss; I'll never be happy here," and when she parts, it is with integrity for both.

Being Grounded Is Refusing Labels

Another form of thinking that can create suffering for you and others around you is thinking in terms of labels. Labels can sometimes be helpful as descriptive words or phrases that are applied to people, places, things, and so on to classify them generally. But, being grounded in truth, you know that labels, especially when applied to people, are often false and divisive, particularly when they are negative. So you reject labels. Here's why:

Look at the labels that might be applied to you. Look at the myriad of classifications: gender, age, sexual orientation, race, religion, nationality, geographical region, birth order, family background, income. How do you feel about them? Are they true? List a few and ***look harder*** at them. You might feel good about certain labels because you think they reflect well upon the way that you see yourself and your image in the eyes of others. You might feel that they are accurate when applied to you. But there are other labels that you do not like. You don't like them because they are false. You don't like them because they are negative. You don't like them because they are too narrow. They may even be stifling. You don't like them because they place you in a group you feel you do not associate yourself with. You don't like them because they are limiting, you are much more dimensional than the label.

When others apply labels to you, it diminishes your individual identity. It defines you in ways that you might not define yourself.

It creates a separateness between you and others that might not really exist and which you do not want because, when you are defined as one thing, it means that you are not something else. So, if you're white, you're not black. If you're conservative, you're not liberal. If you're gay, you're not straight.

Being grounded means you recognize the many problems with labels, starting with the fact that they are inaccurate as applied to many people. Race labels for instance. We, your authors, are considered "white." But what does that really mean? Does it strictly have to do with skin color? Or is it more about ancestry and geographical roots? Is it really helpful as a classification? Does it help to classify a man or woman with five generations of family living in Moscow, Russia in the same group with a man or woman with five generations of family living in Baltimore, Maryland, just because they have the same complexion? So maybe the label white is not helpful. First, from a relational perspective, it serves no purpose except to separate us from other people. We are white, so we are not black, Asian, Native American, or anything else. The label white does have historical significance. We don't need or want to deny that; we just accept that it is true because we are grounded. However, when the label white is applied to us, it actually goes beyond separating us from others; it puts us in opposition to others. That is not a place where we want to be. Secondly, it says nothing to help others understand who we consider ourselves to be. It is not a label we would choose to apply to ourselves, so maybe we don't want the label applied to us by others.

A woman told us a story of her experience in coming to America from Spain. She was asked to declare her race on an immigration form. The categories were confusing to her so she went to the clerk to ask for help. The clerk, looking at her skin color and facial features, said, "You're white, check that."

The lady said, "Well, I'm from Spain, should I check 'Hispanic'?"

"No, that's for Mexicans."

The clerk took the card from her and checked "White."

She said she shook her head and thought, "Isn't a person from Spain considered Hispanic?"

Or consider the racial label, "black." Does it help to classify a recent immigrant to the U.S. from Nigeria in the same group with a man with five generations of family living in Chicago or a man recently immigrated from Jamaica just because they have similar skin color although perhaps many shades different? The recent immigrant, forced to check "Black" might feel proud to do so, but maybe not. They might feel like, by checking a box they just became part of a group that they had not decided they wanted to join.

Or "Asian." Does it help to lump into one group people from such diverse cultures as Japan, Korea, the Philippines, Vietnam, and China. What about India? Pakistan? Mixed racial people? Aren't we all mixed race really? Maybe? Maybe not?

Looking harder at this, you can quickly see how false, or at the very least limiting, it is to apply these labels. Yet our society insists on attaching race labels to people. You are asked to check a box to declare your race many times in your life. Racism does exist. You are grounded and recognize this. But by continuing the practice of classifying people into racial categories that many feel are inaccurate or negative, does our society embrace differences and heal racial division or perpetuate it?

Being grounded, you might check "Other," or nothing at all on forms that ask you to identify your race. You are also well aware that it is not just in the realm of race where labels create conflict. As we discussed, triangling can be a very dangerous form of interaction, and labels are used powerfully to escalate destructive triangling into full-scale divisions between large groups of people.

Here's how that works. A person wants things to be a certain way. Others have different opinions. The person looks for a common label to apply to those in opposition, applies the label, and uses it in making a general statement complaining to others. Just listen to talk radio. You will hear numerous examples daily. The complaints are designed to build a coalition to gain power in opposing, gaining power over, or even wiping out the other. Labels are used as the shorthand for identifying large groups to make it appear as if they are homogenous, monolithic, stripping people of their individualism, lumping them all together as mere members of the group in which they are placed. They also make individual actions and thoughts seem much larger and perhaps more threatening because, instead of being the thoughts and actions of an individual or a small group, they become the thoughts and actions of an entire class of people, unknown in size, without individual identity, and whose bad intentions are easily exaggerated.

Through history, you can think of hundreds of examples where scapegoats are created and oppressed and it begins with assigning a label. Being grounded, knowing that labels are inherently limiting and usually false, you don't use them. You are aware of how powerful—negatively powerful—they are. You stay centered and resist joining in destructive triangling when others use labels.

Being grounded, knowing that labels are inherently limiting and usually false, you don't use them. You are aware of how powerful—negatively powerful—they are.

Being Grounded Is Having Healthy Boundaries —Especially in Relationships

As we have seen, being grounded is having a real love for reality and truth and accepting what is rather than what should be or could be. It also means you are rigorous about truth in not making statements in absolute forms like always and never statements, or in not applying labels to lump large groups of people together. So does being grounded mean that you have no opinions? Does it mean you just give up on trying to have any influence on others? Does it mean that you are a doormat and just accept when others act poorly? It might be easy to rationalize that how others behave is just *who they are* and that the best choice is to accept them and let them be. Well, maybe, but maybe not!

You may be familiar with the Serenity Prayer, brought into popular consciousness by Alcoholics Anonymous (AA). "God, grant me the serenity to accept the things I cannot change, the courage to change the things I can, and the wisdom to know the difference." Being grounded means following the path this prayer encourages. Yes, you accept things and people as they are, but you don't just give up on having influence to create the world that you wish to live in. You discern how you should respond and use your influence, but you don't let your attachment to your thinking about the way things *should* be cause you suffering. It's not trying to control everything, but it's also not being passive. You have healthy boundaries for yourself, your thinking, and how you permit others to affect you.

Being grounded means you accept things and people as they are, but you don't just give up on having influence to create the world that you wish to live in.

Here's an example. You have a spouse who acts poorly according to your idea of what is good behavior. It could be an extreme case. It might not be. But the point is that you don't like their behavior and you wish it would change. If you are not grounded, your thoughts about how your spouse should behave might cause you sleepless nights, constant worry and pain, and give you a gnawing feeling in your gut. Their behavior might also cause you to suffer because they reflect poorly upon you and your family and make you look bad. They embarrass you. However, you are grounded, so it's not like that. You accept them for who they are, but you have influence and the courage to use it. So instead of nagging and complaining to others, you stay centered and directly ask your spouse for the change that you want.

Now comes the hard part. You might not get what you ask for. You might get a positive statement, but then they revert back to the same behavior. You might be rejected entirely. You might get a very angry reaction. We will talk about how to work with bullies and those who are not relational in their interactions with you, but right now we are focusing on you, your internal mind-set, and being grounded. You know that you have choices. You look harder at them. You get clear about what they are and their consequences to the best of your ability. You might leave the relationship. You might stay and continue working in a relational way for the change you desire. You might accept that the change you desire is not going to happen and decide that you want to stay anyway.

It's your decision. You take responsibility for your own happiness and peace of mind. You consider others whom your decision will impact and whether your decision might be good or bad for them. You don't choose to suffer unless you decide that is what you want to do for the well-being of others. Then your suffering has meaning and you are at peace with it. You don't let your thoughts about how your reality should be different than it is consume you with resentment.

However, sometimes your choices might seem very limited or you may feel forced to choose between options that *all* look bad. This may occur in a relationship that you have a great deal of attachment to—with a spouse, sibling, parent, or child—or in interactions with others where you have very little power. Let's look at how you stay grounded in those circumstances. It requires slowing down your thinking and engaging deeply in inquiry about your options. It is similar to what we discussed earlier in being centered as being complaint free, but it is different because now you are looking at your own thinking and how, in staying grounded, you set healthy boundaries and make informed choices. Here's an exercise to help your discernment.

Step One—The Other Person

There's someone in your life who you love, but you are very frustrated with their behavior. Cutting off the relationship with that person might be an option that you just don't want to consider. There are a hundred reasons why you might not want to sever the relationship. You have looked hard at that option and decided it is not a good one. This person is going to remain in your life. Think of that person.

Or . . .

There might be someone in your life whom you don't love, in fact you may dislike them intensely, but they have power to affect you on a daily basis—a partner, a boss, co-worker, political or organizational leader, business owner, neighbor, parent, a sibling or family member. For any number of reasons you might not want to get away from the situation that allows the person to have power over you. Think of that person.

Step Two—The Other Person's Behavior

Think now—What does the person do or not do that you wish would change?

This is not about who they are. This is not about what they should do or could do. Stay grounded. Don't use labels. Avoid never or always thinking. Don't make big factual statements.

Describe the behavior. Be specific. It's not, "You treat me like shit" or "You act as if I don't exist." It is, "I don't like it when you cut in on me when I am talking." This is what is referred to in the field of conflict resolution and non-violent communication as an "**I-statement**"—something you say about yourself, your experience, your feelings. I-statements are useful when you engage in difficult conversations with others, but also as you discern your own thoughts and feelings in your commitment to be grounded. Here you might have multiple behaviors that you don't like. Write them all down.

Step Three—Is it Abuse? If Not, So What?

As you look at the behaviors of the person, you get clear about how you view them. Just the act of being very specific about describing the behavior will help you get clear. You also get clear about how to respond to the other person or why you might choose to stay in the relationship even if the behavior does not change.

In setting healthy boundaries, you ask: Does the behavior hurt me? How? Does it hurt others? How? Is it momentary and you can forgive it and move on? Or is it repeated and ongoing, and beginning to erode your personal or working relationship? If there is abuse, you may want to take a hard look at leaving the relationship. You might ask yourself if the behavior is abusive to you or others you care about, will staying in the relationship only perpetuate the abuse? Maybe, maybe not. You may have many thoughts about why you can't leave the relationship. Now is the time to look at the truth of those thoughts. For instance, if you look at your relationship to an abusive spouse you might say, "I can't leave because it will be bad for the children," or "I can't leave because I have no place to go." Or "I can't leave because my family will never speak to me again." If you look at your relationship to a tyrannical boss you might say, "I can't leave because I won't be able to find another job." Stay grounded in the maybe, maybe not. For each thought you have, ask yourself, "Do I know that is true?" If your reasons for staying in an abusive relationship are based on your assumptions about what will happen in the future if you leave, then, as we said earlier, *Look Harder* and you may find that a path exists for you to set a healthy boundary and leave the relationship.

You *take responsibility for your own well-being*, not subordinating yourself to others who are abusive. If your attachment to an abusive person is so strong that it won't let you do that, then ask, "Why am I so attached to this abusive relationship? What makes this abusive relationship worth staying in? Why?" Answer truthfully from that place of groundedness.

On the other hand, if the behavior is not harmful to you or to others, or does not rise to a level of ongoing abuse, and if you have decided to stay in the relationship, then, ask yourself, "So *now* what?" If you allow the behavior to adversely affect you, then you are responsible for your own suffering. You can make a request for change—staying centered—directly to the person as we just discussed. If the behavior affects others, you can talk to them, being careful not to negatively triangle with them, without complaining, about the change you want. It's okay to persuade and influence others if done in a relational way. In fact, it's one of the best ways to persuade and influence others because it is authentic. That's a lot of what quality dialogue is about. And you can do it with a lot of energy. You do it in a spirit of positive hopefulness about the change that you want, not attacking or judging the other person.

If the behavior is neither harmful to you or to others, yet you are still attached to the idea of leaving the relationship, ask yourself, "Why am I so attached to the idea of leaving? What makes me think it is better elsewhere? Is that true? What will I do? Where will I be? What makes me think it will be better in a year if I leave now? What makes me think the other person is the problem? Is that true? Am I part of the problem? Am I the problem? Is it my thinking that is the problem?" Answer truthfully, from that place of groundedness.

Another option, of course, is that you might just let it go. Accept the behavior and *instead of trying to change them, change your thinking*. If your fear, resentment, or frustration is based on your thinking that refuses to accept a reality you cannot change or do not want to take action to change, then see how you feel when you let go of that thought. You, without that thought, with more peace in your heart, are more relational.

Being Grounded Is Living in the Now—Mostly!

So, as we have seen, being grounded is all about your thinking. Another helpful way to get a handle on your thinking is to consider it from a temporal perspective. How much of my thinking is about the past? How much of my thinking is about the future? Some of that thinking is helpful and necessary, but much of it will lead you to unnecessary suffering and will create real barriers to your ability to be relational in your interactions with others. So, mostly, being grounded means living in the now.[6] The challenge lies in knowing when and how to use thinking about the past and future and in knowing when that thinking is not helpful. Being grounded allows for this discernment.

Winners interested in maximizing self-interest might urge, "Stay away from the past. It'll bog you down, lead you down rabbit holes. It's irrelevant. It doesn't matter. Focus on the future." A relational approach brings a different perspective. Your past may or may not have meaning for your present. Thinking about the past, what happened then, what may or may not have gone right or wrong, and how you feel about it obviously can be valuable to your decision making process today. Experience is a great teacher as they say. You use your past experience every moment of your life on some level of your consciousness. It comprises much of the information upon which you make decisions. The problem is not thinking about the past. The problem is the attachment to thinking about the past when you let it define and limit you, and when you let it define and limit how you interact with others.

---

6 See e.g., Tolle, Eckhardt, *The Power of Now* (1997).

With regard to how you view yourself, being grounded means that you do not let events in your past define who you are as a person. You reject the idea that you are doomed to some fate or that your destiny is fixed because something happened to you or in your family in the past. If you were the victim of crime or abuse, that is not your identity; it is something that happened to you. If you were fabulously successful and famous sometime in your past, that is not who you are, it is something that happened to you. Being grounded, you reject labels for others, so you reject putting labels on yourself. Yes, what happened informs your judgment, but when it is the thought that visits you constantly and limits your ability to experience and live in the present moment, then it is a thought that you want to let pass. So that is what you do. You let the thought pass through your consciousness. You don't feed it. It is just a thought and it will pass. You are not going to let it interfere with your ability to experience the present fully, to focus your attention on the present and make the present joyful—even if you are in the midst of difficult circumstances.

Being grounded means that you do not let events in your past define who you are as a person.

You also do not let your thinking about the past define and limit how you interact with others. You are open to the possibility that others might not do or feel what you anticipate. Maybe they will, but maybe they won't. You do not let events from another person's past define who they are and limit your ability to be ready

You also do not let your thinking about the past define and limit how you interact with others. You are open to the possibility that others might not do or feel what you anticipate.

for them, in the moment, to do something different from what you expect. You do not assume the worst. You are open to being surprised by a change in their behavior.

You also do not let prejudices arising from past experiences with others who remind you of the person in front of you now, limit your ability to be open. This refers to situations where you expect a person to act in a certain way based on some limited information you have about them—their appearance mainly—that makes them like someone else you dealt with in the past. You don't make those blink judgments of a person based on very limited information.[7] You stay grounded in what you know to be true about the person. Mostly, your generosity will give others the benefit of the doubt, expecting a positive interaction with them. Your anticipation of what might happen is not something that interferes with your ability to be relational with the person *now*. This leads us to a discussion about the other form of temporal thinking—your thinking about what might happen, your hopes and fears about the future.

Future thinking is necessary on a very practical level. You need to make plans and it is healthy to set goals. As a winner you probably know how to do this well. Recognizing that you need to do some things before others in a particular sequence is just common sense and that requires some degree of planning. In order to plan you need to think about the future. After just a few moves in a game of chess, if you are a very gifted player, you might say to yourself "checkmate" because you can see ahead all of the moves that you can make, how your opponent can counter, and how the game will resolve itself. That requires future thinking. It is part of

---

7 See Gladwell, Malcolm, *Blink* (2005).

what makes the game of chess fun. But your life and your interactions with others are not a game of chess and you don't want to be so obsessed with the possibilities that your thinking is routinely scattered or paralyzed.

Being grounded means knowing that the variables affecting your future are infinite; unlike a game of chess, however, which has a limited number of pieces and a limited number of possible moves, you have a very limited ability to predict outcomes. So you don't let your healthy planning and goal setting become an unhealthy attachment to a particular vision in your mind of your future. You don't obsess about achieving a certain status level—in wealth, health, power, reputation, comfort, spirituality, relationships, or personal appearance—because that obsession robs you of your ability to find joy in the present moment. You don't get tunnel vision, restricted thinking that gives you relentless drive toward your vision of the future, but excludes or tramples other's well-being. Your thinking about the future may create suffering for others when you impose your vision of the future on them, including your vision of *their* future—particularly for those close to you like your spouse, children, and co-workers.

This does not mean that you give up all your desires. We are not advocating the concept of slavishly surrendering all your attachments. We also are not saying that it is inappropriate to defer gratification and better to seek only immediate contentment. Nor are we saying that it is not good to have goals and work hard to achieve them. Being grounded means that you recognize that most meaningful achievements require hard work and dedication. But when your desires make everything that you do now just a means to an end, with the focus on obtaining something that is not with

> When your desires make everything that you do now just a means to an end, with the focus on obtaining something that is not with you now, something that promises to be better and more fulfilling, then you have subordinated the importance of the present so completely to the potential of the future that the joy of the present is lost.

you now, something that promises to be better and more fulfilling, then you have subordinated the importance of the present so completely to the potential of the future that the joy of the present is lost. Worse, when you use your power to impose your vision of the future upon others, exploiting or abusing them in a way that sucks the joy out of their experience of the present, then clearly you are not relational in your interaction with them. So, being grounded means that even when you are working toward a future goal, you have discernment of what is too much or too little, real or imagined, and remain focused on making the present the best it can be. The journey is as important as the destination. And thus your interactions are not mere transactional means to an end. Being grounded means that when your vision of the future involves the participation and support of others, you moderate your use of power and influence with humility, generosity, and kindness. The future is worth working toward, but not if it means routinely sacrificing the joy in your or other's experience of the now.

You might be saying, "Yeah, but what if my *right now* is miserable?" If you are in very difficult circumstances—pain, disability, grief, or personal crisis—your ability to find peace in the present is greatly challenged. Some of that misery is readily within your power to overcome. For instance, you may be caught up in the past, thinking how this situation occurred and perhaps feeling guilt or remorse. You might be inflicting blame on someone else. You may be caught up in thinking about the future and how it will be limited by how long this emotionally painful situation is going to last. Or you may be out of touch with the true seriousness of the situation and thus causing undue suffering for others with your lack of attentiveness or responsiveness to that situation. Being grounded means you can recognize these thoughts and you are able to discern which ones carry insights and which ones you can let pass while you work to remain in the present, responsive to the now.

If you are saying, "My *right now* is miserable," the bigger challenge lies in the **pain** you are presently experiencing. It feels very real and very present—right now. It is likely magnified and made larger than it really is by the way you think about it, fearful that there is no end in sight, fearful that it will scar you long term, fearful that if you make a move, it will make things worse. But you can transform even these moments—from times when you are miserable and you make those around you miserable to moments when you transcend the pain with your ability to stay in the now. It's not easy, but you can do it by entering into the intensity of the pain, sensing it fully, being curious about it, knowing that the pain and its source are not your identity, that it will pass. A perspective that your soul can endure anything because it is truly immortal draws on your spiritual strength.

Being present in the moment in many cases means—**Just Relax Your Thinking**. That sounds very strange. Especially to winners, when you may have been taught that your thinking, your intellectual ability, is perhaps your most important attribute. And yes, it is important to think and analyze the past to learn from it and look to the future to plan, but, to truly find joy in the present, in the now, you can't be obsessively thinking about the past or the future. Next time you find yourself caught up in an obsessive loop about something that happened or that you anticipate might happen in the future, pause, breathe, have the intention to relax the thoughts, but without the effort to make them go away. Instead, befriend them. Don't fight them. Give them space to flow. Don't wind them up with energy. Focus on your breath where the thinking can coexist, set aside, relaxed. Take another deep breath and focus your attention on what you are experiencing *right then* and make it the *best* experience you can. If you are with someone, focus on being with them fully, listening to them, giving them your full attention. If you are doing something, focus on doing it really well and being grateful that you have the ability to do it. Joy is waiting for you in the moments when you can be in the now.

Joy is waiting for you in the moments when you can be in the now.

Being Grounded Is Being Self-Aware

The final aspect of being grounded goes beyond awareness of how your thinking separates you from truth and reality. It extends to your becoming fully self-aware of all of the aspects of your personality that drive your decision-making and affect your ability to be relational with others. This involves not only awareness of your thinking in particular moments, but the pattern of your actions and thoughts over time as you experience situations. Noticing where you place your attention, habitually, is an important first step as well as an ongoing skill for developing and deepening your self-awareness.

You have tendencies, habits of mind, and go-to strategies for situations that arise. You have an internally wired view of the world, your way of understanding and making sense of it, a view that is both insightful and flawed. You have developed these strategies and views through the course of your life as means to cope and thrive in your environment. Your strategies stem from what you have come to believe you need to survive. They are ancient and primitive and also very alive and in your now. Many of your habits are defense mechanisms that served you well at one time as a child, but no longer do. Being grounded means being aware of your tendencies when they assert themselves in your thinking, recognizing when they are leading you to behavior that is not relational, learning to relax them when they are in excess, and acting deliberately instead of reacting based upon your habits.

Understanding your tendencies and taking action to moderate them requires a strong desire to examine what is true about yourself with honesty and humility. However, it is hard to be objective when you look at yourself. You may not be at all in touch with your patterns of behavior, feeling, and thinking. You may not have any sense of the motivation within you that drives your way of operating in relation to others, or where that motivation comes from. You may think you do not have the powers of imagination needed to see yourself as others see you. So, on your own, becoming self-aware is truly a daunting task, but it is also such a valuable journey to embark upon because it can unlock for you many secrets to your happiness and the ability to find happiness in relation to others.

Understanding your tendencies and taking action to moderate them requires a strong desire to examine what is true about yourself with honesty and humility.

Because it is so interesting and so valuable as well as so complex and difficult, the study of personality has grown through the years and much scientific research has been applied to it. People gain self-knowledge through personality typing systems and assessments which offer to help you identify your type. You probably have experience with one or more of these personality tests or systems—Myers Briggs or Jung, for example—in college, graduate study, or in connection with your work. You may even use one to assess the personalities of your employees, job applicants, or clients. We have used a number of these personality systems in our mediation training practice to help those who are intervening into other people's conflicts to gain insight into the patterns of their own thinking, feeling, and behavior to allow them, as mediators, to understand themselves better so they can be more open to others as they are to themselves. In addition, when people share information about their personality types, it often helps build understanding between them and fosters a compassionate response to some behaviors of others that can, with personality type information, be seen as a result of how the person is wired, rather than judged or passed off as behavior that is "just because they are a (insert epithet here!)."

The study of your personality, *how you habitually function in the world and your habitual thinking* ***and corresponding emotional energy about*** things, people, and situations you encounter, is important because it has a lot to do with how you think, how you think about yourself, how you think about others and how you present yourself to others. But your personality is not who you are. It is not your identity as a person. Your personality is something that—if you learn to practice self-observation by using good clues provided through evidence-based personality typing systems—you can look at objectively. Then you can see when your tendencies are positive influences on your behavior and when they are not. You can see when defenses and coping strategies learned early in life are no longer needed, and you can discern when they become barriers to your ability to be centered and to your ability to relate to others in a healthy way. You can also see when your patterns of thinking are actually mentally created illusions that lead you away from truth and away from being grounded in reality. Ultimately, study of your personality can help you better understand and change your ways of being to be more relational for the sake of your happiness and the happiness of others.

In pursuing self-awareness, we have found that the **Enneagram personality typing system** is very helpful. If you have never heard of it before, you are not alone. Many people haven't, as it is not widely used. However, we have been using it in corporate and educational settings, and Louise has taught it at Harvard's Program on Negotiation, and at the University of Maryland School of Law for many years. There is a large body of writing about it, most notably for us the work of Helen Palmer[8] and her community of Enneagram teachers in the narrative tradition. Louise has studied extensively under Helen's mentorship and has been pioneering the Enneagram method for self-awareness in negotiation and conflict transformation training courses and in mediation practice for over two decades. We have seen time and again its usefulness—offering our clients insights into habits of mind and patterns of behavior for both themselves and others. If you are not

8 See Palmer, Helen, *The Enneagram: Understanding Yourself and the Others in Your Life* (New York, 1988).

aware of it, we would like to introduce it to you briefly and invite you to explore it further.

The Enneagram is unlike any other personality typing system in many ways. First, it has been developed primarily through oral tradition and is not the product of the psychology department of a major university, although there are many faculty members at many prestigious academic institutions such as Harvard and Stanford who fully embrace the effectiveness of the Enneagram. It has a somewhat controversial history in the United States and there are many who look to it to provide a framework for understanding into the realm of theology and spirituality. Also, unlike other personality typing systems, generally you do not discover your Enneagram type by taking a test after which you are told what type you are. Tests do exist, but the preferred process is to listen, face-to-face, to panels of people speaking about their lives who identify with particular type structures as they answer questions and talk about their experience. The Enneagram is more about a person's motivations than their behavior. Those who are practiced self-observers are able, in panel discussions, to talk clearly about their patterns of feeling and behaving, and the corresponding mental preoccupations and the very personalized ways in which their patterns show up. This allows you to see fully a person in all their complexity, helping you to discern for yourself which type you most identify with. That process—choosing your type by observing and listening to panels and self-observing what goes on "on the inside" for yourself—provides valuable insight as you come to appreciate your own worldview, what you came to believe you needed in order to survive, and the worldview of others.

The Enneagram is also unique in that it does not put you in a personality *box* where you are confined and labeled. Many personality systems simply tell you what your type is and then a few things about you that seem more for entertainment than personal growth. The Enneagram recognizes that there are no neat little personality boxes and fully embraces the mystery of each person's individuality. Stated another way, through self-observation, you can find your box so that you can then live outside your box. It takes into consideration the influence of stress and security on personality development and at given times in a person's life. It takes into account that personality behavior, as it appears to others in their dealings with you, can change as you evolve and develop personally on your journey of self-compassion and self-mastery. It allows for all the types to manifest in different ways, as either introverted or extroverted for instance. So it is richer, more complex and also in many ways more difficult to grasp, but therein lies its value. Your type is not who you are, you are much more than a type structure.

> The value of the Enneagram is in the way it helps you to be grounded in the reality of who you are and what your essential nature is.

The value of the Enneagram is in the way it helps you to be grounded in the reality of who you are and what your essential nature is. It helps you work on your understanding of the conditions under which you thrive as a person so that you can lessen your own suffering and the suffering you create for others when you act and think based upon your habits of mind—habits you developed at an early age in order to cope with and make sense of your world. Through it you can gain clarity about your impulses, your patterns of thought and feelings, and the thoughts and feelings that are your preoccupations; and you can learn to detach from them. In developing your consciousness of these preoccupations, you can learn to set them aside. You can learn to see and relax your personal reactivity to situations that trigger your defensive responses. At first sporadically and for short times, but eventually more consistently and longer, you become a different person—a person who has the capacity in the moment to be free from enslavement to their automatics in thought and feeling, habits that drive unconscious living and lead to suffering.

You can also develop a better understanding of *others* and how they function in their type, not so that you can manipulate them or put them in a "box," but rather so that you can *see the reality of your **own** blindness to their point of view and their motivation.* Study of the Enneagram can help you be grounded in the reality that your point of view is not the only point of view and is not the same as another person's and build your capacity for *compassion* in response to the thinking and behavior of others that is outside of your understanding of what is rational or expected. You see that their way of looking at the world, although it may be very different than yours, is equally valid. You see that they, like you, have their own patterns of thought and feeling that drive their behavior.

Study of the Enneagram can help you be grounded in the reality that your point of view is not the only point of view and is not the same as another person's and build your capacity for *compassion.*

Start by visiting *www.EnneagramWorldwide.com.* Through inquiry and perhaps through attending an Enneagram panel workshop, ours or one offered by others in the Enneagram Association in the Narrative Tradition, choose a type that fits for you.

You might change your mind, but eventually one of the nine types will seem to fit best. Encourage those closest to you to do the same for the sake of your enrichment and theirs and your relationship whether it be personal or professional, at home or in the workplace. Then choose from among the wide variety of writing and workshops to help you further understand your type and how you operate in certain situations and in response to others. Build your self-awareness. Practice relaxing your habitual thought patterns by being centered, pausing and shifting your attention to your breathing so you can be more grounded and experience others as they are to themselves and reality as it really is. Learn to recognize your patterns of thought and feeling and impulses and make space in your thinking for maybe, maybe not. Free yourself from the limiting habits of your thoughts and find a new sense of who you are, the authentic you. Discovering this new truth about yourself will allow you to be more open to others as they really are. Relational reciprocity will increase the chance that they in turn will be more open to you, as you really are.

Questions for Your Consideration

In exploring Being Grounded, consider the following questions. If you are not sure about your answers, go back and visit the chapter.

- What's the problem in thinking that someone or something will always be a certain way or will never change?
- How does focusing on what happened in the past cause problems?

- How are you open to versions of the truth that are different from your own?
- What do you do when you feel the urge to pass judgment?
- What deeply held beliefs do you have that limit your understanding of others?
- How are labels that you apply to others helpful, or not, in your understanding of them?
- How do you discern or look harder at someone or something you are unhappy with?
- How do you examine your personality, your tendencies and habits, to gain insight into how they affect your interactions?
- How do you gain insight into the habits and tendencies of others to help you understand them better?

Chapter 6

Being Clear

In looking at what goes into being grounded in reality, we focused on our thinking and being rigorous about truth. Being grounded means that you are conscious of thoughts that lead you to believe things that might not be true or, at the very least, to believe things that you do not *know* to be true. Being clear is also being rigorous about truth, but in a different way. It has to do with *how you share information* with others, or don't share information as the case may be.

Exchanging information is one of the most important aspects of human interaction, particularly when you want to work together with another person, to collaborate, or even merely to engage in simple transactions. Any of the hundreds of books on effective negotiation will tell you that your ability to ask the right questions, listen effectively, and get information from others is key to success. The question, from a relational standpoint, is how do you *share* information with others? What guides you in your decisions to share information or not share it, how much or how little to disclose, and how you use or don't use ambiguity to your advantage?

Being clear might be boiled down to the old adage, "Honesty is the best policy," but is it really that simple? It's all about *transparency*, to use the modern term, and, as with all aspects of being relational, there is much to explore on the ways of being relational as we focus on being clear. There are many factors to consider when looking hard at the ethics of disclosure, non-disclosure, and information sharing. What level of truthfulness and disclosure is ethical, practical, and relational? Or, coming at the issue from the other direction, *Is it ever relational to tell a lie?* When is deception acceptable?

There are a myriad of scenarios to consider, but, with some very limited exceptions, you will know that you are *not* being clear when:

- You intentionally provide false information to another person about something important.
- You receive a request from another person who clearly deserves a response and you answer with silence.
- You use clever words to provide information that is so vague or general that it has no value to the other person.
- You provide information that is intentionally incomplete or evasive in response to requests.
- You routinely bluff and make false threats or demands.
- You make false statements that are unverifiable in order to gain competitive advantage in negotiations.
- You make false statements in order to garner the alignment of others to your side, your view.

- You are sarcastic or use pointed "kidding."
- You are false whenever being truthful might cast you in a bad light.
- You exaggerate claims to a degree where your exaggeration is clear but the truth underlying your statement is not.

You want others to be honest with you. Like so many things, looking at it solely from your own perspective, considering what you need from another person, you don't consider what they might need. Being clear means that you consider *both* your needs *and* the needs of the other person when you exchange information. How you get and give information can be complicated, and maybe even legally dicey, when you overthink it and try to gain power or a bargaining advantage. So, if you want to be relational, get clear on being clear.

Being clear means that you consider *both* your needs *and* the needs of the other person when you exchange information.

How clear do you want to be? *Crystal clear.* Let's see why.

Being Clear Is an Ethic Essential to Healthy Society

Unlike other aspects of being relational that we have discussed so far, being clear calls us to consider behaviors that have been the source of debate for centuries in the field of negotiation ethics. It is specifically part of the moral foundation of many religious traditions including Judaism and Christianity. The Eighth Commandment says, "Thou shalt not bear false witness . . ." In terms of law, virtually all societies consider fraud—harm caused by intentional misrepresentation of material facts—criminally reprehensible. Accusing another of being a "liar" is a serious charge and one that uniformly incites an emotional response. Truthfulness is taken seriously by anyone who deals with others in any context. Your truthfulness or lack thereof is a character trait that powerfully defines you in the eyes of others and in how you view yourself. You need to be deliberate and conscious about any way in which you might compromise truthfulness for any reason.

Truth in our dealings with others is fundamental to our ability to function as a society. Where truth becomes questionable, trust evaporates.

Truth in our dealings with others is fundamental to our ability to function as a society. Where truth becomes questionable, trust evaporates. Imagine a community, a workplace, or family where you could not trust any information that you received from others, where you had to confirm and verify any statement that you relied upon. It would grind to a halt. That is hard to conceive though, isn't it? Truthfulness mostly is taken for granted. Everyone in any functioning community needs to have some confidence that the information that they receive from others is essentially true. *The liar is the exception and he trades on that very fact*—that others will assume he is truthful in his dealings. Being the exception gives power to his lies. So, being clear means that you care a lot about being truthful in your dealings with others because that is also what you expect from them.

The challenge for you as a winner, however, is that you are used to getting what you want in negotiations with others. You have been trained to compete, and deception often gives you a competitive advantage. That is part of winning in a transactional world.

Someone asks you a difficult question and you hedge or even outright lie to keep from disclosing truthful information that might weaken you. You give information that is truthful, but you leave out damaging facts. You let another person base their decision on limited or false information when you know that if they had complete and truthful information they might make a different decision. You do these things for various reasons. You are afraid you won't get what you want. You don't want to look weak or stupid or lazy or careless. You do it for self-preservation and protection of your desired image in the eyes of others. Or, you are just not up for being fully engaged with another person on a difficult or potentially embarrassing topic and so you take the easy way out. And, in a commercial context, you do it for money—to get more, or to spend less. That is just how everyone plays the game, right?

Maybe, maybe not. It depends on your worldview and your sense of *ethics* appropriate to interactions with others. The field of ethics studies human behavior and seeks to define what is right and good behavior according to a defined standard. That standard has a moral component, influenced mainly by religious tradition, but it also is influenced by what is culturally accepted, what is practical and effective, what is considered worthy of criminal punishment under law, or what might prompt a governing professional organization to impose some form of sanction.

Ethical standards differ between individuals, organized groups, communities, ethnic groups, and cultures. It is easy to get lost in trying to identify a guiding principle to help you decide what is or is not ethical. You probably have some sense of your ethical standards with regard to truthfulness, but you may not be fully deliberate about it. You might be making it up as you go along, partaking in the behavior that best serves the situation as it arises. But that just seems too random, doesn't it? What is your guiding principle?

Here is a good starting point: *Consider the perspective of the other person, the one with whom you are exchanging information.* Being relational calls us to focus both on self and other. A deception that might seem reasonable to the deceiver will look very different through the eyes of the person who is deceived. Why is that? Because deception is in essence coercive. No one wants to be coerced into doing or not doing something. Coercion destroys consent. Coercion uses power to achieve its ends. In that way it is neither kind, nor generous as we will discuss later. If a person would, or even might, make a different choice based upon the deception, then the deception has imposed the will of the deceiver upon the deceived. You can be sure that the deceived does not want to be manipulated, even though the deceiver might honestly believe the deception is fair and justified.

Deception is in essence coercive.

So the first step in being clear is to look at the situation from the perspective of the other and ask yourself, "*If I were in their shoes would the deception seem reasonable? Is it within the bounds of fairness?*" It is not easy to think of situations where someone would expect you to be deceitful and think it was fair and reasonable. What comes to mind for you? Anything?

Being Clear About Your Ethics of Disclosure

Taking a look at the ethics of disclosure from the perspective of the other person, you see that, ethically, there is a difference between forms of behavior. Some are more problematic than others. Fraud, for instance, is ethically worse than failing to disclose minor facts or being silent in response to requests for information. Surely, the person on the wrong end of fraud doesn't consider it reasonable or within the bounds of fairness. There is a choice of behaviors related to disclosure, ranging from criminal, to intentionally deceitful, to aggressively competitive, to merely annoying, and finally, to saintly and, some would say, unduly idealistic. You want to know where you are on that spectrum and, at the very least, be conscious and deliberate about your choices as you move around (and possibly down) the spectrum.

So, emphasizing the positive, let's start with what might be called the ***Golden Rule* ethical position**. When a person wants information from you, what would be ideal *for them*?

The ideal for them is for you to *volunteer all information* that you have that might be relevant to their decisions, for all information that you give to be true, and for you to make sure that they fully understand every piece of information that you share with them. From this ethical point on the spectrum, you are making the other person's job in dealing with you as easy as possible. They don't have to ask any questions, but you welcome any questions they ask and respond fully and honestly. They don't have to probe for information. In fact, you work to find out what information they might need for their informed decision-making by asking them questions to explore their needs and desires. They can rely on everything you say, and you might even go to the trouble of providing the evidence and proof necessary for them to have complete confidence in all of your representations. You share with them your analysis of the options and fairness of them. In a commercial context, you might even share your information about cost and expected levels of profit. Furthermore, as information is shared, you make sure that they fully understand it. You use reflections and summaries to ensure clear communication. You even offer to help them with their analysis and decision-making, helping them to test options to ensure that they feel that any decision they make is fully informed and freely made without coercion of any kind. You want to ensure that they have the benefit of all the information you have. This is a generous and kind approach. So when is it a good approach to take?

Maybe not always, but more than you might think. In an interpersonal context, who would not appreciate the Golden Rule treatment from another person? It builds relationship and trust. It leads to agreements that are durable, less likely to break down. Of course, it is not relevant in simple exchange transactions for very small amounts—nobody expects to negotiate the price of an ice cream cone, but you might want to know how many calories it has or what the ingredients are. Information affects your decisions and so you give others information in the same way that you would want to get it. In a commercial context, sellers practicing the Golden Rule ethic generally have happy customers. But in matters of higher stakes business and in our transactional relations with others, there is a problem, isn't there? This approach means you might not get the best deal in a transaction, doesn't it? No matter how you slice it, this approach will cost you *money*. It will hurt your profitability. Right?

Information affects your decisions and so you give others information in the same way that you would want to get it.

Maybe, maybe not. Literally hundreds of business books are built on this premise—that business is a competitive game and you play to win the biggest share of the pie that you ethically can. If you are a player, on behalf of a company that you don't own, your employer expects you to play the game to win. Where you are on the ethical spectrum of disclosure plays a big part in that game. Playing the game according to the Golden Rule ethic means that you are not going to take advantage of any information that *you* know that the other side does *not* know—"*information asymmetry*" as it is referred to in negotiation strategy texts. So, they get to decide the terms on which they will do business with you and they ultimately might be able to decide how much profit they make and you make in the bargain. That doesn't sound good, does it?

> The Golden Rule ethic means that you are not going to take advantage of any information that *you* know that the other side does *not* know—*"information asymmetry."*

But proceeding according to the Golden Rule ethic doesn't mean you are a doormat or in any way a loser. You are grounded and, in setting healthy boundaries, you know that you have options. You can walk away. You can request a facilitated dialogue with the assistance of a mediator in a process that can provide confidentiality and disclosure safeguards. You can tell them what you think is fair and why. You can ask questions seeking full disclosure from them. You can work to verify information that you get. You can be firm in asking for what you want and what you think is right and just. You are willing to do the work necessary to be able to explain and justify your requests. The consequence of practicing this ethic is that you will likely succeed in situations where it is not necessary to deceive the other side in order to gain a positive outcome for yourself. Stated another way, the consequence of practicing this ethic is that you will not succeed in situations where it is necessary to deceive the other side in order to gain a positive outcome for yourself.

Is success valuable where it requires you to use the coercive power of deception? Simply put, in all but the most difficult dilemmas, some of which we will discuss below, being deceptive is not being relational.

You might be saying, "Yeah, but you are asking me to play by an entirely new set of rules, and I am just not ready to volunteer everything I know to the other side." So maybe you want to move down on the ethical spectrum a bit. That is okay. It doesn't mean that you have to start being deceptive. There are ways that you can engage with others and share information that may not meet the Golden Rule standard, but are nonetheless not deceptive. But you have to be very careful in going down this path because it is, as they say, a slippery slope.

Let's start with *compromising on the idea of volunteering information*. There is no deception involved where you conceal nothing and are always truthful, but you only provide information that is requested. It just requires the other side to work and ask questions. That puts the burden on them to ask the right questions in order to get all the information they need. You might hope that they won't ask a critical question that would lead you to reveal information that weakens your position. Think for a moment of situations where you did not get an important piece of information that would have changed your decision because you failed to ask. If you take a moment you can probably come up with many of them—situations where things did not work out as you expected and there was a piece of information that you wished you had asked for, such as when you were excited about buying a new home and you didn't ask about the noise level on weekends, or the neighbors who fight all the time, or the restricted ordinances or covenants. Putting the information-gathering burden upon the other person is not always fair. Your everyday experience confirms this. Laws and rules that require disclosure of essential facts important to consumer decision-making govern commerce in just about any product or service. So, in being clear, while it might not technically be deceptive to decline to volunteer facts, you nonetheless make sure that the other person has material information, the information critical to their decision, especially if you can't reasonably expect them to ask for it. That applies in all contexts, personal as well as commercial. At the right time, you might have to disclose a personal secret, as we will discuss below.

You may draw the line and decide that there is some information that you can fairly declare off limits for disclosure. Again you have to be very careful about this because you may end up withholding information that would cause the other person to make a different choice in dealing with you. If they make an information request that you consider out of bounds, asking you to reveal confidential information or information that you feel is truly "none of their business," then you explain to them why it is a question you won't answer. For instance, if you own an auto repair shop and a customer asks you how much you pay your mechanics as an hourly wage, you might answer that your wage rates for workers, while relevant to the customer's interest in making sure that the markup on service work is not too high, is proprietary to your business and something you choose

You may draw the line and decide that there is some information that you can fairly declare off limits for disclosure.

not to disclose. If the customer does not like your response then they can choose to go elsewhere with their business. You may lose a customer but you won't resort to using deception.

Similarly, *you don't stonewall with silence* when information is requested. Silence usually isn't deceptive, but it is also rarely helpful to the other person. Stonewalling will inflame the suspicion of the other person. It is likely to make them assume the worst. Stonewalling is a sign of disrespect and disregard for the other person's interest in getting information. It is simply bad practice and escalates conflict. It can also be a form of bullying, which we will discuss later. Being relational means you are engaged, you don't stonewall. At the very least, rather than remain silent, you can respond to a request for information with a statement explaining why you can't or don't want to provide the information requested. "Thanks, sir. I am not inclined to do that, but I will consider it and get back to you before the end of the week."

Stonewalling is a sign of disrespect and disregard for the other person's interest in getting information.

Moving further down the ethical spectrum there is a wide range of *competitive negotiation behavior*. Being clear means that you *don't* engage in it even if it might be expedient, with very few exceptions as discussed below. You don't use *clever words* to say things that might sound good, but are so vague or incomplete as to be almost meaningless. That, unfortunately, is the tactic of many politicians and what might be called "lawyer talk." You hear it every day—big broad statements or carefully hedged positions, couched in opinion but sounding like fact; persuasive statistics that appear to support a conclusion, but which have a questionable basis in reality. Statements that might, if they are carefully parsed, technically be true, but which imply something that is not true. Tactics of debate and rhetoric that seek to shade, hide, and obfuscate the truth. Anytime you are trying to persuade others, hoping that they will believe something that you know is not based in reality and which omits facts that, if made clear, would cast things in a very different light, you are manipulating and coercing them. That's not relational. Coercion is force and an abuse of power as we will discuss ahead in connection with being kind.

Likewise, you don't make *exaggerated claims* with the idea that your exaggeration is so obvious that it can't be taken seriously. This is referred to as "puffing" and even if it might be considered harmless or even expected in a negotiation, it seeks to influence the behavior of another person with information that is not true. They do not know where the truth stops and the exaggeration begins in your statement. The same holds true with bluffing, false threats, sarcasm, and deception related to your bottom line.

Once you go down the path of deception, you have broken your relation to the other person. You are no longer in the realm of quality interaction and dialogue and you are headed for a crisis in your interaction with them. Which leads us to the next reason for being clear—in the end, it is not only better for them if you are clear, it is also better for *you*.

Being Clear Is a Better Way for You

Practicing deception often does more harm to you than it does to the person you seek to deceive. It may seem to give you an advantage

Practicing deception often does more harm to you than it does to the person you seek to deceive.

in the short run, helping you get something that you want, but at a high cost. Once you deceive, you have walked the plank. You have put the noose on your own neck. First, there is damage to your own personal sense of integrity. As a winner, you view yourself as a person who is worthy of respect. When you deceive others, you risk losing your self-respect. You look in the mirror and see a person you don't like.

Maybe you don't care. Maybe you feel that your behavior is justified because "everybody does it," or it is "how the game is played," or it is for a "higher, more important, purpose." Perhaps you feel that you have the power to deceive others because there is nothing they can do about it. But think about what the falsehood does to you. Now you have to be very careful about how you deal with the other person. You may have to weave deception on top of your deception in order to prevent discovery of the original falsehood. Lies beget lies as they say. You need to keep track of what you have represented to the other person, how it differs from reality, and how you can ensure it is not discovered. You have to keep track of the other deceits you have to put forth in order to prop up the first deceit. It is usually a losing battle, especially if you deal with the person often and the falsehood is about something important. In the very least you have to exert great energy being very careful about your misrepresentations, very clever to make sure that they are statements that can't be verified. It's time consuming. It's stressful. Is it really worth it?

What if the falsehood is discovered? You have done great damage to your reputation. You now have a person who no longer trusts you and who will deal with you differently going forward. You need to do a lot of repair work to put the relationship back on track. You will need forgiveness, and their kindness might not extend far enough for them to offer that to you. The relationship may be broken forever as the other simply chooses no longer to associate with you. That can be devastating in personal contexts like family and marital relations. In commerce, you probably have lost a customer or a vendor. They are likely to move on to the next person they can do business with. And there are usually others who are also adversely impacted by the deceit, breach of trust, and resulting fracture. Each loss weakens the strength of the system, whether that is the family, the enterprise, or the community.

You have also hurt yourself in the sense that you have damaged the level of trust that exists in the community that you are part of. Your deception may prompt others to be deceptive in retaliation or because they now think it necessary behavior in a corrupt society. You have participated in making the community just a little more coarse, a little more dog-eat-dog, and indirectly you contribute to your own suffering. It is easy to see how this applies to important relationships. This also applies even where, in a random, anonymous transaction, you have deceived someone whom you will never deal with again. So, without regard for the other, merely for your own sake, you can see that being clear is vital to your health and well-being.

Dilemmas in Being Clear

Despite our best intentions and desire for personal integrity, however, life poses dilemmas to us, situations where deception might seem the right and moral choice. Ethicists have devoted much thought to these situations, weaving elaborate hypotheticals to test moral constructs related to truthfulness.[9] We can't begin to address them all here, but we would like you to consider a few. In being relational, it is important to look at these situations because, as discussed above, allowing any deception to enter into your interactions with others is very risky. We want to help you be conscious and deliberate when and if you ever choose to stray from the Golden Rule ethic.

The classic dilemma involves *deception in the face of evil.* The evil party seeks information from you. The information you provide could aid them in their efforts to do evil. Silence might be an option, but often it is not because it would betray another innocent person. Silence might also expose you to grave harm. Time is of the essence. There is no real opportunity for dialogue. Nazi storm troopers come to your door searching for Jews, one of whom is hidden in your attic. Silence would be an admission. A lie is necessary to protect your friend. So you deceive and you are successful. You take a risk to protect someone who was innocent, and yourself as well. You've done a good thing.

But most circumstances are not so narrow and clear cut. First, you have to be sure that you are indeed dealing with others who have evil intentions. Second, there is no time for dialogue. Third, you have to be sure that your truthfulness would aid evil. Fourth, silence is not an option. Each of these criteria is difficult to satisfy. Being clear means that you consider them carefully before you engage in deception.

First, evil is often in the eye of the beholder. Remember negative triangling, demonizing others to build coalitions, and its

9 See e.g., Augustine, St. "On Lying" and "Against Lying," in R.J. Deferrari, ed., *Treatises on Various Subjects* (New York, 1952).

destructive power in communities. You are careful not to judge another as justly deserving deception simply because you judge that they belong to a group of which you are suspicious. Certainly it's not okay for Democrats to lie to Republicans, or vice versa, just because of policy disagreements even if the feeling is that some in the other group are truly evil. Being grounded, you are very careful whom you label as "evil."

But sometimes you are not sure about their intentions. You might suspect that they have bad motives and think that the safest course is to treat them as if they are evil until you know better. Fundamentally it is a question of trust. Better safe than sorry as they say. However using deception is rarely safe as we discussed above. *So when in doubt and when time allows, you take the first step in being relational: you engage.* You ask questions. You listen carefully. You reflect what they said using their words. You get information. You are present, attentive, and interested in them. Sometimes the pressure of time and the level of perceived threat from the other will affect your judgment here. Is there a threat of imminent harm? Deception to prevent harm when you have a gun in your face is obviously appropriate. But the use of deception just because you think that the other might have a gun, or might get one in the future, is different. Since deception is a use of coercive power, as with any use of power, being relational calls you to prefer dialogue and use coercive forms of power only as a last resort.

Since deception is a use of coercive power, as with any use of power, being relational calls you to prefer dialogue and use coercive forms of power only as a last resort.

Next, consider whether truthfulness will truly aid the evil or whether it is just to serve your idea of a better course. Using deception to serve a "higher purpose" that you believe in is not deception to prevent giving aid to evil. For instance, it's not okay to distort facts in order to gain approval of others for some course of action just because you think that course is the right path. Think "weapons of mass destruction are stockpiled in Iraq" and therefore the United States needs to invade. This deception is a shortcut, a lazy way of trying to build consensus. It is contrary to all notions of informed decision-making through quality dialogue. Yes, there are situations where secrets need to be kept in order to ensure security. You don't reveal your ATM pin number to anyone, right? You have no duty to reveal information to anyone who has no legitimate interest in knowing it. But again, deception is a last resort.

It's not okay to distort facts in order to gain approval of others for some course of action just because you think that course is the right path.

Most of the time in a difficult situation, *silence is an option.* Silence rarely reveals anything. In order for silence to reveal information, the inquiry has to call for a yes or no answer, and the person seeking information has to assume that you are acting out of self-interest. As we discussed with regard to stonewalling, when a response to a question is silence, the questioner will usually assume the worst. So, to choose a mundane example, if the question is "Did you do the dishes?" Silence means no. Or, in a relationship, "Are you cheating on me?" Silence means yes. In these examples, separated from the other elements of the Nazi storm trooper scenario, your best course is honesty and full disclosure according to the Golden Rule ethic. Usually there is at the very least the option to say, "I can't say," and explain why. Whenever possible, choose that option in lieu of choosing to deceive the other person.

When and if you do disclose, you are thoughtful about what you disclose, conscious of the impact that disclosure can have on yourself, the person seeking the information, and others not part of the conversation, but who will be affected by the disclosure. This brings us to a special category of dilemmas in disclosure—secrets and confidences.

Secrets and Confidences

When there is something about you or your past that you do not want to disclose to another person, you may decide to keep it a secret. Secrets are things about you that you withhold from disclosure. Confidences, however, are different from secrets. Confidences involve your keeping *another person's* secret or the secret of a group or organization of which you are part. For personal reasons, secrets might be difficult to deal with, but they do not necessarily pose great challenges for you in being clear. Confidences, on the other hand, can create dilemmas that are very thorny because they can put you in a position where you are torn between several conflicting interests, your self-interest, the interests of the person who wants to keep the secret, and the person from whom the secret is kept. Let's look at secrets and confidences a bit closer.

Confidences can create dilemmas that are very thorny because they can put you in a position where you are torn between several conflicting interests, your self-interest, the interests of the person who wants to keep the secret, and the person from whom the secret is kept.

You have secrets. Everyone does. You may keep them for a number of reasons that are perfectly justifiable. For instance, the details about your sex life with your spouse is something that you might not want to disclose to others. Maybe you do. That is your business. If there is violence and abuse, it might become someone else's business, but normally it is not. Details about your habits in sleep, personal care, choice of reading material, and so on, are things that you might want to keep secret.

Privacy is an important value and essential to good society among people with widely different tastes, norms, and practices. Your discretion in creating boundaries around your personal thoughts and personal life, and your respect for the same boundaries created by others, help you to coexist peacefully in a crowded and hyper-connected world. Being relational, you are not a busybody and you expect others not to be busybodies.

> Being clear means that you don't withhold a secret from another person when your failure to disclose the secret would hurt them.

But being clear means that you don't withhold a secret from another person when your failure to disclose the secret would hurt them. The physician's creed of "first, do no harm" applies. You find the right time, place, and way to tell someone your secret if, considering their perspective and everything you know about them, you feel that they need to know your secret. That might be a complicated conversation that you want to have with a lot of care. Perhaps the other person does not want to know your secret. You can test that by asking them broadly, "Are there questions you have about my (health history, sex life, quirky habits, personal needs, family history, run-ins with the law, financial troubles, job losses, substance abuse, and so on)?" In most contexts these things might be totally out of bounds for general conversation, but in some they might be critical—intimate personal relationships and the formation of business partnerships for instance. You might be surprised when someone says that they don't care to know.

Being clear means you don't use deception to coerce another person. It also means, as we discuss below about being gently honest, you don't allow your failures to become secrets by covering them up or hiding them when they happen. You disclose important information to others immediately as a rule. In this sense, your decision process in disclosing a secret is no different than other situations we have discussed in being clear. Unlike other situations, however, disclosure of your secrets might be particularly painful for you because it might cost you a relationship or cause embarrassment or humiliation. Being relational means caring for yourself and others so, in caring for yourself and in the context of the relationship, you might discern that keeping a long-held secret is best. You might discern that disclosure would hurt the other person and your relationship more than keeping the secret would. That is a choice you might make out of kindness to yourself and to them. That is your decision. Being relational means you make that decision very carefully.

> Being clear means you don't allow your failures to become secrets by covering them up or hiding them when they happen. You disclose important information to others immediately as a rule.

You also are very careful about *how you deal with others' confidences*, the secrets you hold that are not yours alone. You may have a special role in relation to another that requires you to keep confidences absolutely confidential. If you have professional duties—lawyer, priest, doctor, therapist, or mediator for instance—you may be called to hold confidences even though you know that another person, who does not know the secret, would very much want to know it. In these professional contexts very limited exceptions to confidentiality exist and the professional generally is called upon to disclose those exceptions before the person tells their secret to the professional. Think imminent threats of violence or serious criminal injury and elder or child abuse. Otherwise as a professional, you keep the confidence even if it might put you in an uncomfortable position of stating why you cannot address the situation even when you think it might be helpful to others to know. And if the confidence is about whether or not the professional relationship even exists, you keep the confidence even if it might put you in an uncomfortable position of having to evade inquiries or even resort to outright deception in order not to disclose the confidence. In the context of a special professional role, that might still be within the boundaries of being clear. As a professional, you make those judgment calls as part of your duty to the people whom you serve.

Confidences become more difficult however, when they are held in relationships that do not involve a special professional role—for instance when you serve as an employee or ordinary "rank and file" member of a group. It could be in your role as an employee, member of a family, member in an association or club, or in your role as John Doe, citizen. In these roles you feel a general duty to be loyal to the group. You might also feel a personal obligation to hold secret from others certain things that you know about the organization that others do not know. When you believe that it is not right to keep certain information secret from others, you face a dilemma. Being relational, you may decide you must disclose. *How* you disclose is also part of being clear. You must decide whether or not to "blow the whistle."

Whistleblowing is the much-debated[10] situation where a person cries "foul" on an organization that they are a part of. It is a dilemma because the whistleblower is often torn in many directions—between:

> Whistleblowing is the much-debated situation where a person cries "foul" on an organization that they are a part of.

- their own desire not to suffer retaliation;
- needs of others who might depend on the whistleblower as a family income provider;
- needs and reasons of the group in keeping the secret;
- the impact (positive and/or negative) that disclosure of the secret will have on members of the group that they are part of; and
- the impact (positive and/or negative) that disclosure of the secret will have on others who are outside of the group.

Needless to say, often the situation is complicated. So in being clear, you have to make some tough decisions. Loyalty is not the issue. That is an oversimplified perspective on the problem. No group can demand blind loyalty. That is fascism. So, you weigh all of the interests involved. Being relational means *considering both self and other*. In the same way that blind loyalty is not the issue, neither is blind self-sacrifice, ignoring the consequences to yourself and others close to you. You have options; you look harder at them.

First, you consider where you are in the hierarchy of the group and the urgency of the need to disclose. If it exists, you go up the

10 See e.g., Bouville, Mathieu, *Whistle-blowing and Morality*, Institute of Materials Research and Engineering, Singapore 117602 (2007).

chain of authority to ask them to disclose the secret. You seek to persuade them about the importance of disclosure as you see it and, as we discuss below with regard to kindness, you use your power wisely. You engage by first listening to understand fully why the group does not want to disclose the secret. You stay centered and don't complain to try to build a harmful coalition; you don't negatively triangle. You go to those with responsibility for the decision. Imminently threatened serious harm might require you to go right to the top quickly, but you are grounded and look hard at whether the urgency you sense is just your rising internal reactivity or whether the stirring is a cue for something that is real and true. You may have more time to deal with the issue than at first you think you do.

As you engage with others in the group about whether or not disclosure of the secret is the best option, you regularly look at all the consequences for everyone involved. There are no simple rules here. The situation might be made more complicated when non-disclosure may bypass criminal consequences or increase the likelihood that bad behavior may occur again. The situation might be extreme—the disclosure might be a fatal blow to the organization, the threatened retaliation might be extreme, keeping the secret might result in severe harm to others. Hopefully you will never encounter a nightmare scenario. Being clear, being relational, just means that you make decisions consciously in a fully engaged, centered, and grounded way. You are discerning and proactive considering the consequences to the best of your ability.

You might decide to blow the whistle by going to an external authority—the press, police, and so on—if internal authorities are not responsive and you discern the need for disclosure is paramount. If you do, you are prepared for the consequences and accept them. Some organizations have elaborate systems to encourage whistleblowing and to protect whistleblowers.[11] To us, these systems are good solutions for organizations and help reduce the whistleblower's dilemma. Even with protections, the whistleblower, however, may still suffer consequences. Being relational, you have thoughtfully considered the consequences and you accept them.

You may decide to leave the group and let the issue go. You may decide to stay within the group and let the issue go. Maybe not. That is your decision and being relational demands no particular outcome.

Being Gently Honest

Finally, there is the concept of gentle honesty. Being clear doesn't mean you are harsh with the truth. Kindness, or at least a desire to not be hurtful, guides you in sharing information. You are familiar with the concept of "white lies," untruths stated or allowed to exist in the interest of compassion for others. These fall into two categories of untruth: subjective and objective. The first category is not even deceptive most of the time. It involves your stating an opinion that is not one you truly hold. You might do this frequently to prevent hurting the feelings of someone you care about and most of the time it does not affect their decision-making.

For instance, at dinner your spouse might ask you, "How do you like this dish?" Your true opinion might be that you think it is okay but not great, or even that it is not good at all. In the interest

11 See CRS Whistleblower procedure, http://secure.ethicspoint.com/domain/media/en/gui/12748/whistle.pdf.

of your relationship, however, you say, "It's good, honey, thanks for making it." You can think of a hundred similar examples and the point is that you are not being honest in the sense that you say exactly what you think in terms of your subjective opinion, but rather, in the context of your relationship with the other, you choose not to be harsh with your opinion. You think to yourself, *I am grateful for this meal and the hands that prepared it.* It does not involve any need for informed decision making.

As we discussed above with regard to the Golden Rule ethic, looking at the situation from the perspective of the other person, what would they more highly value, blunt honesty or a gentle "white lie?" Being relational, you decide this in the context of your relationship and what you know about the other person and their sensitivity. In some cases blunt honesty will be just fine. The other person may well appreciate it. They may have even asked you for it. You provide it from a place of center and groundedness, factual and not puffed up. In others, you know they will be more receptive to a gentle approach in giving them your true opinion or you may never express your true opinion at all. You may follow the advice of "If you have nothing good to say, don't say anything at all." In these situations you also ask yourself "*Am I being overly critical, stingy with my goodwill, or ungrateful; or, on the other hand, would my opinion give useful input to the other person that they would appreciate? Am I using my false opinion to try to coerce the other person, to get them to do or not do something that they might not otherwise do?*" If you are grounded, you will have this kind of inner conversation right in the moment. You may realize that you are using your false opinion just to avoid conflict. You avoided what could actually have been a healthy exchange and could have deepened your relationship if you had known how to engage in it. Being gently honest means that, in giving your opinion, you consider the relationship context and you consider the power and influence you have. As we will discuss ahead, you are kind in how you use that power. That's not being deceptive.

Being gently honest means that, in giving your opinion, you consider the relationship context and you consider the power and influence you have.

On the other hand, misrepresentations about *factual* matters, even in the context of relationship, are deceptive even if your motives are compassion and care for others. Being clear means that you are very careful about factual untruths offered because you judge that others "can't handle the truth." A few examples illustrate how thorny this can be.

Grandma is fatally ill and you don't want to upset your children so you tell them that she is fine and will get better soon. She dies. Later they discover that you kept her fatal illness from them and they resent you for it. You thought you were being compassionate, but that is not how they see it.

Your mother suffers from dementia or Alzheimer's and she keeps asking you when her husband, your father, will be coming to see her. He has been dead for many years. You told her that once when she asked and she got very upset, re-experiencing real grief. She asks you again and you tell her, "I am sure he will be along sometime soon." Then you change the subject. She never discovers that you were not honest. Your deception is purely compassionate.

In both of the above examples the *compassionate justification* for your deception is grounded in your judgment about the lack of capacity in the other to cope effectively with the truth—first because of young age and second because of mental illness. You have to make the judgment about whether in certain circumstances it is compassionate to be untrue. Being clear means you do so deliberately. You keep in mind the consequences of your lie of being discovered. In the Grandma scenario above, when the kids get older if they discover that they might have been able to spend more time with Grandma had they known the truth, or to tell Grandma that they loved her before she died, you really may have broken trust with them. They may wonder what else you deceived them about. You also must discern whether your deception is truly out of compassion for someone else or, on the other hand, whether it is out of your own self-interest, such as conflict avoidance, ego, or enabling.

For example, there is some fact that you believe will upset another person. You also believe that they do not know it. Maybe you have some responsibility for the situation. You did or didn't do something and you would rather they did not know about it. You betrayed them somehow. Maybe you have no responsibility at all like the Grandma or Alzheimer's scenarios above, but you just don't want to be part of experiencing the emotional scene that you expect to occur when the truth is revealed. Being clear means that you don't allow your interest in avoiding responsibility for your actions, or your desire to avoid emotional scenes to justify deception in the name of being compassionate. This can be very difficult.

Being clear means that you don't allow your interest in avoiding responsibility for your actions, or your desire to avoid emotional scenes to justify deception in the name of being compassionate.

If you have responsibility, then being clear means you

take responsibility and accept the consequences of your actions. If you betrayed a spouse or lover with infidelity or even a business partner with disloyalty or failure in performance, you tell them the truth immediately and clearly. You don't even let the fact become a secret that you would have to live with and perhaps disclose later. Even though they might get upset, you know that any deception would only be a time bomb in your relationship waiting to blow up. And you can't be sure what their reaction will be. Being grounded tells you not to assume that you know what the future will hold. You may think that it is compassionate to withhold the truth, but in reality you are only doing so to dodge the consequences of your actions. So you don't do it.

Even if you don't have responsibility for the situation, being clear calls you to consider whom you are really serving with your "compassionate" deception. If you are just trying to avoid an emotional scene because it will upset and bother *you* and be difficult *for you* to deal with, then you are not being compassionate. You are being stingy with your emotional energy, your patience, and your care for others. No question, being in the middle of someone else's emotional pain is not easy or pleasant. It is an act of generosity, giving of yourself.

Truth telling is an essential part of being relational. Quality dialogue requires the exchange of truthful information. That may mean putting yourself into difficult conversations. When you engage from a place of center, you are grounded in reality and you are clear about your

> When you engage from a place of center, you are grounded in reality and you are clear about your disclosure ethics, you are strong enough to be vulnerable. It takes courage.

disclosure ethics, you are strong enough to be vulnerable. It takes courage. But if you are engaged, if you enter and stay in the conversation, if you remain centered and grounded, and are clear, then you will be able to have amazing quality interactions and the kind of quality dialogue that will lead to breakthroughs, resolutions, reconciliation, and healing. From there, *you can go even further in creating lasting positive outcomes that reverberate, that are paid forward, that foster connection, reconciliation, peace, and justice.* You do that by being generous, humble, and kind.

Questions for Your Consideration

In exploring Being Clear, consider the following questions. If you are not sure about your answers, go back and visit the chapter.

- What is your approach to deciding whether or not to disclose information to another person that you think they would want to know, but that at the same time might upset or disturb them?
- What is your approach in deciding whether or not to disclose information to another person that you know they would want, but which might not be favorable to you?
- How does silence in response to a request for information create problems?
- Why is your ethical approach to disclosure important in your personal relationships, organization or community?
- When do you say, "That's none of your business?"—Or maybe a more diplomatic version of that, "I need a boundary here and

do not want to share that information with you." And why might you say that?

- What keeps you from fully disclosing important information?
- What is your approach to disclosure to others of your secrets?
- What are "white lies"? And are they ever okay?
- What is your approach to whistleblowing and disclosure of confidences?

ORANS

Part Three:

The Three Ways to Lasting Change

We have a motto that is a core concept for the work we do as mediators—***Amazing things happen through quality dialogue***. We truly believe that, and we have seen it over and over again. Even in the midst of intractable conflict, when we help people with being engaged, centered, grounded, and clear, *then* shifts occur and little by little people become stronger and less self-absorbed. These shifts are the transformation to openness. The byproducts of the four ways to quality interaction are openness and receptivity to others and the situation. You are able to see the perspective of someone else, and give and receive recognition. The innate desire to mend the fracture in relating that exists, to restore the connection as a fellow human to another, motivates people to work through conflict. Our practice of mediation, focusing on the quality of the interaction, believing in the capacity of people in conflict to find solutions and answers they can live with, and completely respecting their right to self-determination, is referred to as the **transformative approach** to mediation. The term transformative is used because the process aspires to foster positive change, to transform the experience of conflict.

Being relational also has a transformative goal. But it goes beyond just seeking a positive change in the quality of interaction between people in conflict. *Being relational means seeking a positive change in the quality of relating between you and everyone you come in contact with* and it strives for lasting positive change. It starts with you and the choices you make in your daily life.

> As a winner, you have power to create positive change in your family, in your work, in your community, in your world. Everything you do matters.

As a winner, you have power to create positive change in your family, in your work, in your community, in your world. Everything you do matters.

Doing your part to promote quality interactions goes a long way towards building relationships with those you care about, and towards making a connection with those you encounter randomly in your day. Doing your part in this way, however, does not necessarily mean that you are fully being relational. If you are effectively using the ways to promote quality interaction—being engaged, centered, grounded, and clear—just to get what you want, get your way, promote yourself, maximize your take of resources, and, above all, *to win*, then you are not being relational, you are just being a very skilled transactional negotiator, a wolf in sheep's clothing. In order to be a force for positive transformation, a person who makes a positive difference, a person who inspires others, who serves as a role model, then you will need to look harder at how everything you do and think and say affects others around you. You will need to ask yourself, "How do I make the world a better place?"

As a winner, you have the power to make a difference . . . will you?

Our belief is that you make a difference by being relational, and the frontier for you to explore beyond promoting quality interaction involves your being generous, being humble, and being kind. We will look at what each of these ways of being means and *why these transformative ways of being are critical to the future of our species on this crowded, hyper-connected planet.* We want to take a good hard look at that and ask you to come along, remain open, and then decide for yourself what your choices will be.

ORANS

Chapter Seven

Being Generous

What is your experience when someone is generous with you? Does it make you feel good? Does it elevate your sense of dignity, self-worth? Does it inspire you? Do you feel grateful? The answer to each of these questions about your experience with generosity is probably *yes*. However, if you really *look hard* at them, the answer is maybe, maybe not. Your experience depends on many factors related to you and to the other person—your thoughts, feelings, and actions; their thoughts, feelings, and actions. Being generous involves someone giving and someone receiving, but the experience of the recipient might not be as positive as the giver might assume. Similarly, for the giver, the experience might have a negative side. Or it could be very positive on both sides of the equation. It depends, right? Our theory is that being generous is your participation in making the world a better place. But we are not going to assume that is the case. In being grounded, we want to examine that assumption closely. Why be generous? First let's look at that and then we will look at what it means to be generous in a relational way.

Why Being Generous Might Look Too Risky

Being generous is a leap of faith. There is no denying that you are taking chances when you give away anything of value to another, even if it is only your time.

Being generous is a leap of faith. Like us, you might have a moral or religious tradition that tells you that giving is good, but in practice it is full of risks for you and for others you care about. There is no denying that you are taking chances when you give away anything of value to another, even if it is only your time. It might be easy for an independently wealthy recluse who lives alone in a humble shack to talk about being generous, but it is very different for a person who has family and responsibilities. When you have responsibility to others in your family, when you are a parent, you have to think first about your family. Will they have enough? Will they be safe? Will they be healthy and cared for? Will the children be educated and prepared for life? How can I be giving anything away when I can't be sure that I will have enough to care for my family?

Your responsibility within your family unit is a legitimate constraint on your generosity, isn't it? You can't do something that would put your family at risk. Even if you don't have family responsibilities, the future is uncertain and you can't be sure how much you will need in order to make sure that you never go hungry.

If you are a winner, you may not want to take any risk that you might suffer a setback somewhere down the road that would force a change in your comfortable lifestyle. So, yes, you want to be good, but you feel kind of stuck. You have to continue to accumulate as much as you can in wealth and devote the vast majority of your waking moments to earning the money you need to maintain your lifestyle. You do your duty in paying taxes and in giving what you comfortably can to charity out of your excess. That is the safe and prudent course financially.

There are other risks to consider. For instance, the risk that your generosity would be wasted or, even worse, that you will set yourself up to be taken advantage of or ridiculed for being foolish. The money you give might be used for things that are not good, instead of necessities and things that really make a difference in a good person's life. You may have no control over how your gift is actually used by the person who receives it. And, if you give support to others, then they might come to expect it. They might not be grateful at all for your generosity. They may even come to depend on it and feel entitled to it. You could actually be contributing to their dependence, which isn't good for you or them. You might be giving to someone who doesn't even deserve it. They could be mean and violent and greedy and just using you or the system to get stuff for free.

Then there's the risk of the precedent you set with your generosity. If you are an employer for example, and you give one employee a raise out of generosity, then you can expect others to be coming and asking for the same treatment. If you give a customer a break on their bill or a tenant a break on their rent, you can expect others to come and ask for the same deal. Next thing you know, your generosity has snowballed into something much bigger. It's costing you a ton of money and people are thinking that you are a push-over, a soft touch, and maybe even a bad business person. If you are working for a profit-driven boss or private investors who want you to perform well for the company and you give a customer a break on price or pay more than you have to for a service, then you've set yourself up to be criticized and possibly fired. Likewise, if you spend too much time with charitable work, you are also putting yourself at risk with the boss. Being generous is risky. Is it worth it?

Why Being Generous Is Good for You and Others

Now consider the other side of the equation in weighing your decision. First is the value of generosity simply in the context of your dealings with others and the relative ease of transactional interactions. When you are generous, you easily break negotiation deadlocks. Since you aren't trying to get the last dollar on the table and maximize your gain, resolutions are quicker and your dealings more pleasant and less stressful. You part with a smile and a handshake. There was no winner and loser. You were generous, you left money on the table, and the other person was happy not to get squeezed, which made you both feel good.

When you are generous, you easily break negotiation deadlocks.

That brings us to another great reason for being generous. It physically and emotionally makes you feel good. You get an emotional rush out of it. Some people who feel this rush more strongly actually come to crave it and seek it often. Studies in neuroscience show that even compulsory giving, like paying taxes, activates portions of the brain that release dopamine, providing pleasure and warm feelings as if you yourself received a reward.[12] Especially if your generosity meets with approval from the other person and they offer you a smile or some other gesture showing their good feelings toward you. You are also more likely to live longer and more contentedly.[13] What's more, if the approval of others is important to you, it probably makes you look good in the eyes of others who are not even the recipients—neighbors, peers, and colleagues. You may get some recognition from them for being a generous person.

You also internally give yourself recognition. Your sense of self and your value in the world is given a boost. Generosity, particularly in the form of volunteering time to help others, is regularly used to help people suffering from depression to break out of their state of self-absorption and negativity in how they view themselves.

There are other benefits for you. You build goodwill with others to whom you give. They are happy to receive a gift and may repay your kindness someday. What goes around, comes around. If you pay a kindness forward, it may be paid back to you. When you are generous with clients and customers, they are likely to return. You create positive karma that you yourself are the beneficiary of. Generosity is contagious and when you are generous, others feel empowered to be generous too, and you start a ripple of generosity that can quickly become a wave.

---

12 See Svoboda, Elizabeth, "Hard-Wired for Giving," WSJ Online (August 31, 2013).

13 See Firestone, Lisa, "Generosity, What's in It for You? Compassion Matters," *PsychologyToday .com* (November 24, 2010).

If you are generous to people who work for you, then you have happier, more satisfied workers who might be more productive, more positive in their dealings with other workers, and less apt to quit. You reduce costly turnover in employees. You also have made a down payment on peace and harmony in your community or workplace. When you are generous, you reduce the likelihood that others will feel oppressed and exploited, and they are less likely to create unrest. This makes your community safer and happier and a more pleasant place to live and work.

Being in a place that is happier and safer is good, isn't it? Your community is an extension of you, just like your family. You are generous because you feel a sense of responsibility to others in your community just like you feel responsibility to care for your family. You want to be proud of your community and how it treats people who live in it. When your generosity helps lift up the lives of those around you, then you know that you have contributed to reducing misery and poverty and shame, and to fostering well-being, dignity, beauty, and connection. You have been a part of respecting the dignity of all families, not just your own, and their desire to live and work in peace and in conditions that are healthy, safe, and even aesthetically uplifting.

> You are generous because you feel a sense of responsibility to others in your community just like you feel responsibility to care for your family.

So, if you look at it from a purely personal and even self-centered perspective, it's totally worth it to be generous, isn't it?

Being Generous in the First Instance

So, if you have decided that being generous is a way of living that you want to adopt, we want to help you explore how your generosity can have the greatest positive impact. We all know that generosity involves giving, but there are different ways to give aren't there?

To start, there is **altruistic giving,** which involves giving with no expectation of anything in return. Our perspective is that really, given what we know about the ability of giving to create a positive ripple effect, we rarely give with no expectation of anything in return. As we discussed above, we fully expect our giving to create positive outcomes that indirectly will benefit us, albeit not in a transactional sense. We know there is energy in the act of giving, and there is an energetic reciprocity. The issue is not the *expectation* of anything in return, it is more the *asking* for something in return. Altruistic generosity means you are not asking for anything in return.

Altruistic generosity means you are not asking for anything in return.

Communities are experimenting with this kind of giving and doing it in ways that are countercultural for those of us who live in competitive societies. For instance, there is the Seva Café in Ahmedabad, Gujarat, India, a restaurant where there are no prices on the menu only this footnote at the bottom of the check: "Your meal was a gift from someone who came before you. To keep the chain of gifts alive, we invite you to pay it forward for those who dine after you." Patrons pay whatever they want. In the restaurant's own words, here is the concept:

> *At Seva Café, we serve with the spirit of "Atithi Devo Bhava" which translates to "The Guest is God," a deep and ancient Indian view that honors each guest with reverence. We're all used to the concept of offering a meal to family or a friend who visits our home, but at Seva Café, we extend this generosity to a stranger we don't even know. The guests are told we trust them to accept this gift and pay forward the generosity so that this experiment can continue.*[14]

The Seva Café is thriving. Why? Judging from all of the positive attention it has gained, it is because it inspires people to give. Then there is the Aravind Eye Care Network, also in India, which provides life-changing cataract surgery to millions for free.[15] Patients pay nothing or whatever they can afford and wish to pay. Aravind is rigorously efficient and manages to be financially viable by performing a great volume of high quality procedures at a fraction of the cost incurred by traditional hospitals. Those who pay for services subsidize those who do not. Making these ventures work is greatly challenging, but their success surprisingly proves that, in the right circumstances, radical generosity can not only lead to feelings of good will in a community, it can be part of a sustainable model for enterprises that provide valuable service to communities.

You might be saying, "That is all well and good in India, but it would never work in America." You might be right. But the Seva Café and Aravind Eye Care Network do give us an intriguing model

---

14 See *http://www.movedbylove.org/projects/sevacafe/* (2014).

15 See *www.aravind.org*; also Rosenberg, Tina, *A Hospital Network with a Vision*, New York Times Online; *http://opinionator.blogs.nytimes.com/2013/01/16/in-india-leading-a-hospital-franchise-with-vision/?_php=true&_type=blogs&_r=0* (2013).

of generosity to explore that we ask you to consider adopting as a way of being relational. They both give in the ***first instance***. They don't maximize the first transaction with the idea of giving back later. *They give up front with faith in the good that will come back to them later.*

The American model of giving is very different. Generally speaking, it works like this (and winners know this model well): You work and try to gain as much as you can from your work. You take care of your needs and the needs of your family. You contribute to the general well-being by paying taxes and doing other required duties as a citizen such as living within the boundaries of the law. Then, if your current needs are met, if you have enough saved up to ensure your future financial security, you show your gratitude by giving your excess time and money to your favorite charities, making sure to take the allowed tax deduction. Did we get any of that wrong?

Let's be clear. There is nothing bad about this kind of giving. It is, after all, giving, and we don't want to look down our noses at it. We don't want to be snobby about generosity. We don't want you to think that if this is what you are doing then you are not being a good citizen, a good person.

How would it feel to be generous in the first instance, to give now without waiting to make sure that your gift will not take needed resources away from you, without waiting to see what you might get in return, without waiting to make sure your gift will be appreciated, used well, and received by a person worthy of your generosity.

But *how would it feel to do it differently?* How would it feel to be generous in the first instance, to give now without waiting to make sure that your gift will not take needed resources away from you, without waiting to see what you might get in return, without waiting to make sure your gift will be appreciated, used well, and received by a person worthy of your generosity. It might feel good to give now without waiting. It might inspire others to do the same. It might create a positive wave of change. You could make a difference with your generosity *in the first instance.*

Break the American model down and look at its component parts and you will discover many opportunities to be generous in the first instance. Step one in the American model is working and trying to gain as much as you can through your efforts and hard work. It is based on the idea of competition as the best and most efficient way to allocate resources amongst people. You know, however, that the American system has a way of giving winners like you the power in many contexts to take more and give less. Being generous in the first instance means that you look for ways to use your power to do the opposite—*take less and give more—daily*, without waiting to see if it is wise to do so from the standpoint of preserving your resources and maximizing your wealth, comfort and security.

You know the expression, you may have grown up with it in your household as we did in ours, "From those to whom much is given, much is expected." For you as a winner, on the receiving end of plenty, whether by pedigree, family background and good connections, or hard work and good health, or even just plain good luck in the right place at the right time, being generous means knowing and believing that you have enough. You live in abundance. Your existence is not about striving for more in terms of wealth, comfort, recognition or security.

Being generous means knowing and believing that you have enough.

Being Generous in the First Instance with Employees

Some challenging situations in being generous involve how you deal with people who work for you. Say you own a company and, being generous, you would like to give the employees a raise. The CFO says the company can afford it, but you don't know what the last half of the year will bring, so you don't. You're not sure how the investors will react to your doing something that you don't have to do. The year ends up well and in December, you tell your employees that you are going to give them a bonus. You gave, but you didn't give in the first instance, you waited and that changed the nature of your generosity. Why? Because you could have given raises six months earlier. The company had the means to do so. By virtue of your waiting, your employees do not have the benefit of six months of additional earnings and income in ways that could make their lives better. And when you put the raise in the form of a bonus, it changes the context entirely. It's as if it is now a gift from you, something the employees should thank you for, as if it was not earned by them. Sure, it's still generous; no one is denying that giving bonuses and sharing wealth with employees in the form of bonuses is a good thing to do. It's just not being generous in the first instance.

Also, consider the example of an employee who is asking for a raise and she hasn't even been with the company a year. But she is asking now so that it will be in place when she gets to her first-year anniversary date. You consider the request. She is a good worker, but she is slow and it seems as if she doesn't pick up on what she has been trained to do very easily or quickly. You like her well enough. What she does, she does well. She doesn't do her job as well as her predecessor, but you will definitely keep her on board. She has a very positive attitude and always is there on time and ready to work. You are considering a four percent raise since you brought her in on the low end, giving her time to learn. But, she then told you she's asking for a twenty percent raise! She says she needs to move out of her parent's home and she needs more money to afford her own apartment. What do you do?

You might think that a twenty percent raise is out of the question. She certainly hasn't earned that. What you are paying her now is the going market rate. You know, however, that whatever the "market" may bear, the market is oppressive when it comes to wages. Child labor laws, eight-hour work day laws, and workplace safety laws exist because historically employers the world over who have power will exploit their employees. You are not an exploitive employer, so you won't use the market to justify turning down her request.

But then you might say to yourself, "But if I raise her that much, then what about the other staff? They'll find out and I'll have to do it for everyone. She will want a big raise every year." Being generous means you aren't held back by precedent setting.

Being generous means you aren't held back by precedent setting.

You want to be generous in the first instance, but you might also need to have some dialogue with her about it. Being relational, you welcome quality dialogue in working through issues with others. You don't want to make her beg. You respect her dignity. You want her to understand the risk you are taking. If she really needs the money to move out, if she continues to be conscientious in her work, and she understands that you won't be able to raise her twenty percent next year or anything even close to that, then you give her the raise. You didn't just blithely say yes, you gave it careful consideration, but you were inclined to be generous in the first instance. In the transactional sense, to use a figure of speech, your thumb was on the scale, but in favor of *giving*.

Just to round out this idea fully, here's another example. You are the CEO of a company owned by a private equity investor group. They come to you with a proposal—if the company outsources labor to contract staffing firms it can save millions in labor costs for unskilled workers. What does that mean? It means you would lay a lot of people off, maybe break their union, and many would be rehired at lower wages by the staffing firm. The employees will lose benefits. The equity investors argue that there is nothing illegal about this and that it will greatly improve the company's bottom line and make it more competitive in the marketplace because it will have a lower cost structure. It will give the company more flexibility because all hiring and firing of workers will be done by the non-union staffing firm and the company will be able to get labor on an as-needed basis, never having to worry about laying people off because that will all be handled by the staffing contractor. Furthermore, competitors are doing it and the company needs to follow suit. The investors demand this change to help them achieve their goals for return on investment and in building the equity value of the company.

You are in a dilemma. It is no skin off your back financially, in fact it might result in your earning even more than you have, but you don't want to do it. You believe it is not only wrong and completely in opposition to your desire to be generous, but you also think it is bad business. You believe it will cost the company in terms of labor unrest, turnover in workers, harm to the quality of customer service, and bad publicity. What do you do?

You engage with the investors. You use your best relational skills to explain fully your views and support them with evidence. You hunker down and do the hard work needed to try to prevent the company from taking the path of ruthless competition. You are generous with your efforts. You know that it is an uphill battle to argue in the face of the investors' spreadsheet analysis. You know that it's not easy to prove good that might come in the future as a result of choosing the path of generosity. But you are sacrificial in your giving, putting yourself on the line to protect the employees who may not have the power to protect themselves. That's the kind of generosity that can make a lasting change in the lives of others. That's you making a positive difference.

We need courageous, generous people to step up and be a positive force to help those who are exploited by extreme practices in pursuit of profits.

This kind of thing is going on out there in the marketplace every day. We need courageous, generous people to step up and be a positive force to help those who are exploited by extreme practices in pursuit of profits. Being generous means you *reject exploitation.*

Being Generous in the First Instance as a Mind-Set

Being generous in the first instance is all about changing your mind-set. You are a winner. You have enough. You will always have enough. You don't have to maximize your take. This applies to you, your family, and organizations that you are involved with.

With regards to yourself, that means you live modestly. We are not saying that you should sell all your worldly possessions and give them all to the poor, but if you want to do that, it would be exceedingly generous. How you live reflects your humility, which is essential in being relational as we will discuss below. You want to live a good healthy life. You will have to decide what that means for you. But your focus is not on accumulating anything—houses, cars, clothes, jewelry, and so on. Since you are not gathering more and more, you have more that you can give now. You can leave a good tip for your waitress—twenty percent at least. You can put more in the poor box at church. You can give now to any charity when you see its need.

It becomes a bit more challenging, however, when you extend this concept to your family context. You might have responsibility in your family as a parent, spouse, or child. Now it's not just about you and what you think is acceptable as a good and healthy lifestyle for yourself. There are *other* people involved who may have *different* ideas. Your spouse might want a bigger house, a new car, and kids going to private schools. Your parents might want you to have a high-powered career. Your children might want to go to an expensive university. You will need to engage with them. Once again, being relational calls you to dialogue. You explain your hope and desire that your family's generosity will have a great impact on your community and the world. You ask them to join you in discerning how your family can be generous. Through the relational process of quality dialogue, you make a decision together to be generous. It might take time. You are generous with your time and efforts because you believe in the power of your generosity.

We are not saying you should change your spending and investing, that is a personal decision based on your family's circumstances, but maybe, before spending or investing, you might ask: Do we need all the insurance policies to protect us from potential losses or should we shed some of them and give more now to others? How comfortable should our retirement be and when should we plan to retire? Is it necessary to go to an elite college or will the state university meet educational needs? Are private schools really needed? Do we need a second home? Do we need elaborate vacations? Is it important to drive a new car? How much is good to spend on our appearances, on clothes, and on jewelry? How much is good to spend on recreation? Do we need to eat out so regularly? How much do we spend on alcohol?

You might be thinking, "Wow, you are going to turn me into a big stick in the mud!" Maybe, maybe not. It depends on your mind-set and the mind-set of your family. If you feel like you are taking away from your joy of living because you are giving too much to others, then your desire to be generous might only be sowing seeds of your future resentment. It was not giving from a place of centeredness, groundedness, and clarity. If your giving, and your family's choices which allow you to give, make you feel joyful, then you are on the right track. Talk to your family about it. Have a family meeting. You will find the answers through dialogue. Amazing things might happen.

If your giving, and your family's choices which allow you to give, make you feel joyful, then you are on the right track.

Finally, think about *bringing the generosity mind-set to organizations* of which you are a part. We discussed how this might apply in a private company, but consider how it *also applies in the context of a non-profit.* Many non-profits function just like a family does with regard to finances. There are current needs and desires and there are future needs to consider.

Here is a typical story. The organization starts with a charitable mission. It is beautiful and good. People are excited about it and there is an initial burst of creative energy. It hires some staff, most of whom are willing to work for low wages because they are believers in the mission and grateful for employment. The organization gets some grants and donations. As it becomes institutionalized, its mission changes. The people working there want to keep their jobs. They want to make more money. They want benefits and a retirement plan. It becomes focused on growth and survival, and the charitable mission, though still beautiful and good, is not what occupies the minds of the people working there. They decide that an endowment would help. Building a nest egg to generate investment income to fund the operations would provide the stability that the organization needs. Nicer offices would enhance the reputation of the organization, maybe even a new building. Suddenly the focus is, "We need to raise more money! How about a capital campaign?" So they create a development department and now a sizeable part of the organization's staff is devoted to fundraising.

You can probably see where this is going. The organization has lost sight of its mission. It has opted in favor of institutional growth, financial security, and service to the financial needs of its leaders and workers. It is no longer able to be a "give first" organization. It risks losing its soul as a charitable entity, becoming just a for-profit business in non-profit clothes. The only difference is that it doesn't have shareholder owners gaining wealth from its efforts. This is what has happened and is happening in many educational, healthcare, social service, religious, and civic organizations. It doesn't have to be this way.

If you are involved with a non-profit charity, you can bring the generosity mind-set to it by encouraging it to *focus on service to its charitable mission* and not on institutional growth and stability. It can *use volunteers* to the greatest extent possible. It can *stay community-based* and resist efforts to make it grow and become institutionalized. It can stay in donated office space and keep facilities costs to a bare minimum. It can give its ideas and methods freely to other organizations seeking to do the same good work in other communities. Being generous means that you want a *thousand* flowers to bloom, not just a few big ones.

Being Generous Is About More Than Money

As you can see generosity is a big topic. You might be saying, "But I work my ass off and live paycheck to paycheck. I can't afford to be generous." Yes you can. Because generosity has to do with a lot more than just money.

Giving of your *time* is a powerful way to be generous. Yes, that involves volunteering to help in your community, but it is more than just that. You take the time to listen and be engaged with another person. You are patient in listening and being present. You aren't in a rush to get away and move on to the next thing. You do not duck out of and avoid difficult conversations. You pause and offer a kind word to someone in many of the moments in your day when you might rather just go on and keep to yourself. You let someone else go ahead of you in a queue or in a parking lot, you hold the door for someone. You know that your little acts of generosity can have a big positive impact.

You know that your little acts of generosity can have a big positive impact.

You also give of your *spirit.* You offer a smile to another person even though you might not be feeling well. You give them the benefit of the doubt in how you view them. You are willing to take the risk that you might be taken advantage of or pushed aside because you want to assume that others are kind and honest even if you suspect they might not be. You don't keep track of wrongs done to you by another and you don't carry a grudge.

You *take the risk that you will be rejected* or even ridiculed. You accept that others might be offended by your generosity, taking it as an insult, rejecting you with a glance or attitude that says, "Look, I don't need your help." You don't let that deter you or wound you in a way that prevents you from being generous in the next encounter. You remain humble. It's hard to be truly generous if you aren't humble, if your pride leads you to give only because of the puffed up sense of self-importance that you feel.

Similarly, being generous in a humble way leads you to *step aside and allow others to shine.* Like when you have poured your heart and soul into an organization for many years. You enjoy the power and recognition that you have earned through your service. But you know others would like to have a share in that too. So you allow them to take over and you give up your position. Maybe you stay involved in a supporting role. Maybe you just move on to another project. It's okay, your service was not based on the power and recognition you gained from it. You did it in a spirit of generosity and because you cared about the mission of the organization.

Your *forgiveness* is another form of generosity in spirit. As we will discuss ahead in being kind, it doesn't mean that there are no consequences to bad acts, but you don't treat someone like a pariah just because they did you wrong somewhere along the line. You give them another chance. You treat them with dignity. You might even engage with them and try to help them understand the hurt you experienced, giving them the opportunity to say they are sorry and make amends. We see this often in mediation. It is an act of generosity for someone to take the time to sit with a person whom they consider a bad actor. Good things often come of it. But also we see how people often, understandably, would rather just write someone off and have nothing further to do with them. It's easier that way, right? Being generous means you prefer to engage in a relational way rather than just walk away.

You give your efforts, your energy, your ideas, your knowledge, your power. There are so many ways you can be generous. When you do a job, you strive to do it well. You don't cut corners or just try to do the minimum. When you are involved with others, you bring energy to the group. You are engaged. You aren't a lump on a log or a wet blanket. You don't withhold your ideas and knowledge from others. You share them even if it means stretching yourself to overcome shyness or hesitation. As a winner you have power, you give it to help achieve positive outcomes for others, and you generously choose not to use your power when you can

As a winner you have power, you give it to help achieve positive outcomes for others.

see that to do otherwise would not be kind. You do that because you care for both yourself and for others. That is what being relational is all about.

Being Generous Is About Connectedness

Ultimately, your generosity isn't motivated purely by self-interest and your knowledge that giving to others, in the end, will benefit you. Rather, your care and generosity come from the way that you view others in relation to yourself. Living relationally, you don't view them as competitors or anonymous actors who, by necessity, you have to deal with in your efforts to get what you want. Being relational means that you feel a connectedness to others. What affects them negatively or positively affects you in the same way.

Being relational means that you feel a connectedness to others. What affects them negatively or positively affects you in the same way.

What does this connectedness feel like? **Here is an exercise**. It helps to *think of some group of people* whom you already have connectedness with and go from there. It might be your family, your tribe, or your church. For us, as for most, the most powerful connection is with our family. Now *think about a relationship* that is particularly important to you and that you are actively involved in right now, not sometime in the past. In the family context it might be your spouse, partner, parent, your child, your brother, or sister. Don't think about a relationship that might be broken. Think of one that is healthy and strong now—today. If you can't think of one, then you have work to do in becoming relational or you might just need to "look harder."

Are you generous with that person? Stay grounded in reality and look harder at yourself, your actions, your motivations. *How* are you generous with them? Think of the ways. If you can't be generous with someone whom you are in a strong and healthy relationship with, it is hard to think about being generous with others.

With that person, what **motivates** you to be generous in all of the ways we have discussed? Make a list. Don't stop at one or two. List at least 10 motivations.

Here is ours—thinking of our daughter Paula: We are generous because . . .

- We love her
- She is truly flesh of our flesh
- We feel responsible for her well-being
- We have known her forever
- We know her heart is good
- We admire her, she's smart and kind and beautiful
- She is kind and good to us
- We want her to always be kind and good to us
- She is a fun person to be around
- We want her to be happy
- We want her to have a good healthy life
- We want to inspire her to be good
- We trust that she will make good use of whatever we give her
- She is grateful when we give to her
- We are hopeful for her future and want to help her
- When we give to her, it makes us happy
- We want to model generosity for her so she might also find joy in giving

- We want her to be happy with herself so she will attract and choose a good person who is happy as well to spend the rest of her life with

Look at the list you just made and start to think about another person close to you. Are there motivations in your list that might apply to that person? Are there other motivations? All *these motivations are your experience of connectedness* to that person.

Now think about people not as close to you—from people you know well to strangers you encounter in the course of your day. Think about in-laws, ex-spouses, and ex business partners. Think about the clerk at the supermarket or the homeless person on the street corner in the city. Are there motivations that might apply to them? Being relational means that you *look for these motivations*; you are in touch with them as you decide how to interact with others. You may have to ***look harder***. From a place of centeredness, groundedness, and clarity, you find a motivation that you can tap into, increasing your feeling of connectedness to that person, increasing your desire to be generous, and knowing that your generosity will make a difference.

Questions for Your Consideration

In exploring Being Generous, consider the following questions. If you are not sure about your answers, go back and visit the chapter.

- How often are you generous with people before you know if you are going to get something from them in return?
- What are the risks for you in being generous with your time and resources?
- When do you give without asking for anything in return?
- What is your approach to negotiation in business for yourself? On behalf of others? Can you leave money on the table?
- Looking harder at yourself, what motivates you to be generous?
- What is the American model for generosity, and how could it be different?
- When you are in a position of authority with employees or otherwise, what is your approach to being generous in response to their needs?

ORANS

Chapter Eight

Being Humble

We just saw how important it is to look for motivations in connection with your generosity. We want to stick with that concept—examining motivation—and how your motivation, which drives your actions, affects how your actions may or may not be relational. Being humble has to do with your motivation. When you interact with others, do your actions—what you do or don't do, and what you say or don't say—come from your desire to respect others and care about them? Or are you motivated by your desire to promote yourself, draw attention to yourself, or gain accolades? Are you motivated by the appearance of being humble? Are you motivated by self-protection and fear? Are you motivated by your desire to win and maximize your advantage?

Being humble means you *recognize when your actions are ego-driven* and based in pride, and you choose instead to look for motivations based on care and respect for others and yourself. You take a balanced approach serving both yourself and others because you view both yourself and others as equally part of something larger. Humility involves your struggle with desires that are deep within you for strength and security and recognition. For winners, recognizing our ego-driven motivations is perhaps the most challenging part of being relational. It is what defines servant leadership and is a critical element in the ability of many leaders to achieve exceptional results.[16]

Keeping a balanced focus on both self and other is the challenge. You will know that your ego is asserting itself and your pride is taking over when:

- Your problem or need is more important than the other person's.
- Your problem or need is an excuse to be rude, pushy and demanding.
- You believe that you deserve special treatment that others don't deserve.
- You look down on others, judging them to be lesser than you in some way.
- You see yourself as a big wheel and others as cogs.
- You aren't grateful for what you have; you deserve more.
- You don't check your work.
- You don't accept any criticism or input. You're sure you are right.
- You are complacent with things as they are and satisfied to "just get by."
- You're a free rider.

16 See Collins, J.C., *Good to Great: Why some companies make the leap . . . and others don't* (New York, 2001), identifying humility as a distinguishing attribute in Level 5 leaders.

- You are a doormat and let others literally walk over you without speaking up.
- You give to get, expect a public thank you, and crave recognition.
- You encounter a needy person and assume you know what they need and how you can help.

So is being humble just about avoiding the behaviors and attitudes associated with pride? Maybe, maybe not. Humility is not something you can just put on like a coat, not a way for you to *act*. Rather, true humility comes from within. It is just the way you *are*. You know your place and you see the truth of your personal significance. You need to cultivate it in the depths of your essence—in your very soul, and if you do, it will bring out the best in you and everyone around you. Let's look at how you can grow in humility.

True humility comes from within. You know your place and you see the truth of your personal significance.

Being Humble Is Being Grateful

Humility starts with being grateful. If you are a winner, you live in abundance; you have much to be grateful for. You have probably heard that one of the secrets to happiness is having an *attitude of gratitude*. Just Google it; it's a very popular concept. What does it mean? It means that you recognize that there is so much good in your life and it did not come to you because you earned it or deserve it. Yes, you may have worked hard and you strive to be good, but that did not bring you sunsets and flowers and breezes in the trees and friendly smiles from others or so many other simple joys in your life. They were gifts. Being humble recognizes that just about everything good in your life is a gift. This recognition is a key to finding joy because unlike things that you earn or buy or take, there is no transactional aspect to receiving a gift. You can't get less than you deserve because you deserve nothing. So whatever you receive is something to celebrate and be joyful about—it's gravy, it's icing on the cake, pennies from heaven, it just fell into your lap and came to you. As the recipient of many gifts, you have no reason not to be joyful.

Your challenge is to ***see*** all of the gifts. You may take many of them for granted. Gifts in your life come from many sources. Some come from the universe, from God—or whatever you might think of as the ultimate creative source in the universe—like the wonders of nature and the miracle of your body and mind. Being grateful means that you, as a winner, do not take it for granted that you have a good sound body and mind. So you take care of yourself and are compassionate to others who have physical or mental challenges. You do not take it for granted that there is good air to breathe and clean water to drink and so you take care to be a good steward of resources and of the environment.

> Being grateful means that you, do not take it for granted that you have a good sound body and mind.

Other gifts come to you by *inheritance from those who went before you*—like everything that makes your life more comfortable and easier than the life of your ancestors. You do not take it for granted that you had parents to love and support and care for you. So you make the best of the opportunities given to you by your parents and if you receive the gift of children in your life, you love and care and support them and you do your part to help other parents do the same. You do not take it for granted that you have systems that bring you fresh water and affordable food and limitless access to entertainment and information and learning. So you work to improve on them for the next generation and to take those systems to other parts of the world where they might not be quite so well developed. You do not take it for granted that you enjoy centuries of beautiful music and art and so you support those who create beauty in music and art for future generations. You do not take it for granted that you live in a country that is free and democratic and organized and safe and so you want to pass that along to the next generation and make your world an even better place for them.

Some gifts come to you *from the generosity of others who give of themselves* in ways that enrich your life. You do not take for granted the efforts of those around you in the common effort to make your community a better place—those who volunteer or share their gifts of talent and wisdom, such as giving of their time at your children's schools, at your church, in your neighborhood association, and those who just do their job with an eye on doing quality work. Humility means knowing the reality of your place in the world, your place in the grand scheme of things, and that starts with the realization that you are the recipient of many gifts.

You do not take for granted the efforts of those around you in the common effort to make your community a better place.

Take a hard look at your life—what are you grateful for and how do you show it? One of the practices we find helpful is to engage in a quick go-round at the dinner table each evening with a question, "What are you grateful for today?" Often the answer might just be, "Good food!" But other times it goes much deeper, "Time with my brother on our rides to school," or "My parents' forgiveness." Give it a try. Recognizing all of the gifts in your life—every day—helps you find joy and keep your difficulties in perspective. Your attitude of gratitude will lift you up and your joy in turn will lift up others.

Your Posture in Meeting Others—As Brothers and Sisters

Lifting up others sounds great, but in reality it is likely not the norm in many aspects of your life. As a winner you know how to compete and your success in many ways depends on your ability to promote yourself and gain recognition from others. Your intuition might tell you that humility will not serve you well if you are trying to get ahead. Your instinct might be to do all you can to stand out from the crowd, to get noticed, and show your superior abilities or efforts to others. You want to be an important person, someone who matters. This is part of life in your crowded competitive world, where you live among a mass of strangers. So you feel the need to make a statement and assert your individuality. As a winner, your urge for recognition and attention are probably strong. Your desire to win, to have the upper hand, is strong. That's how you made it. So you want to meet others in a way that lets them know that you are a force to be reckoned with, someone to be respected.

How you meet others in your interactions, however, has consequences. As you encounter others, several things are possible.

You can meet them in a superior, dominant posture. You can meet them in an inferior, subservient posture. You can meet as equals, or perhaps as brothers or sisters.

Winners often have a way of *assuming a dominant posture.* They are superior. This character trait is called *hubris*, excessive pride. It works as a strategy for getting their way. It helps them *sell* themselves and their ideas to others. Maybe it even extends beyond themselves, like when it ensures that their children go first, get the first opportunity, as extensions of themselves. They may even bolster their sense of superiority with a condescending attitude, a put-down, a demeaning joke, or withering criticism directed at someone else. They are more important. In dealing with another person, their need is more important than the need of the other. Their problem, their burden, their health issue, the pressures of their life, or whatever else they might experience as their plight or privilege justifies their action toward the other person in getting what they want. Their rudeness, aggression, dismissiveness or lack of caring is often excused by others who expect this behavior from people of power and privilege.

But as we said, assuming this posture as your way of being with others has consequences. The saying goes that *you can't raise yourself up by putting others down.* There is a reason why the downfall of the character full of hubris is a classic theme in literature. Seizing a dominant posture in relation to others may work in an anonymous transactional world, but eventually it also *leads to isolation and even self-destruction* in a community as others reject you and your domineering ways. You might get to the top, but it will be lonely there and chances are you won't stay there long. Leaders with an ego-driven, self-promoting, dominant style often can achieve short-term results, but those results are not lasting because the foundation of the organization, its people, invariably rejects the leader.[17] Ego-driven leaders sow seeds of discontent leading to sabotage, apathy, and abandonment. People will undermine the leader, do only what is needed to get by and cover their backside, or just quit working with the ego-driven leader entirely.

Ego-driven leaders sow seeds of discontent leading to sabotage, apathy, and abandonment.

Then there is the opposite end of the spectrum, the practice of *false humility*, a subservient posture that is *just another form of ego-driven pride*. You adopt the attitude of, "Woe is me, I'm just not worthy." Or "I really did nothing, it was all the efforts of others." Here you are just fishing for attention and recognition to soothe your insecurity. You are self-absorbed and assert the supremacy of your neediness. Since others quickly see this posture as false and self-serving, just like other ego-driven behavior, it leads to rejection and isolation.

So the preferred choice in being humble might seem to be approaching the other in a *genuinely subservient posture*. While it is often preferable in the eyes of others, it probably is not natural for you as a winner. Yes, "How may I serve you?" is a good question for you to ask, but being humble does not mean you are there to be a doormat, walked on and stepped over by others. Being humble does not mean you are a slave—to anyone. And yet, clearly there are many situations where you show deference to others. Everyone has bosses to serve and elders to respect. Everyone lives

17 See e.g., Cain, Susan, *Quiet: The Power of Introverts in a World That Can't Stop Talking*, (2013, New York).

in communities with some form of hierarchy of roles where the respect of others for each person within the hierarchy is essential to good order and a healthy functioning society. A company doesn't work when the employees don't respect the CEO. A community isn't safe when citizens don't respect law enforcement.

Respect for authority is part of humility and being relational. Quality dialogue, without complaining or triangling, as discussed earlier, is also important. So, with respect for authority, you practice the ways of being relational involved in conflict transformation—being engaged, centered, grounded, and clear. You engage with authority respectfully, with humility, through dialogue.

Does that mean you try to meet others as *equals*? Maybe, maybe not. "As equals" is just too evaluative. It is not necessary to be equal to others. It is not necessary to demand equality or try to define what equality means with regard to others. Sometimes they are your peers; sometimes they are not. Sometimes you need respect for your authority; sometimes others need respect for theirs. *A better way to meet others is as brothers and sisters.* You are fellow human beings, inhabitants of Earth. Humility is not being superior and dominant or inferior and subservient to others. It is not demanding equality to others. It values both self and other. It is, "You are my brother. You are my sister. I am your brother. I am your sister."

Humility is not being superior and dominant or inferior and subservient to others. It values both self and other.

What does it mean to meet others as brothers and sisters? If you have a healthy relationship with a brother or sister, then you know. Think about your actual brother or sister—the person in your family who has the same mother you do. We are not talking about your "brother" or "sister" in a religious community. *You don't think of your brother or sister as your equal; that's an irrelevant concept in the context of family.* They are just a person in your family who is like you in many ways and also different than you are. You care about them and want what is best for them because you share a bond with them, a bond of family, a bond of love. You don't judge them to be lesser or greater than you. You might not like their behavior or their attitudes, but your actions toward them are always in the context of your family relationship, which you want to be strong and good. So you are relational in the way you deal with them, especially in conflict.

Being humble means you recognize that every person, including yourself, is a unique combination of qualities and none is "better" than any other.

Similarly, being humble means you recognize that every person, including yourself, is a unique combination of qualities and none is "better" than any other. You know that any standard by which you might judge them to be superior or inferior to you—wealth, intelligence, appearance, and so on—is looking at only a mere fraction of the fullness that makes up that person. You know that if you knew them from childhood like a brother or sister they would be much more to you than these qualities so you resist looking at others through these lenses. Instead, you are open to the idea that you and the other, together, are part of something larger, an extended family. The family bond means that you value your relationship to the other person just as you would to a brother or sister.

This quality of meeting others in an attitude that is neither superior nor inferior can be captured by the physical stance of ORANS, an open posture toward others, with an openness to what may transpire, believing it can be good. Jump to the very end of the book if you are curious about that.

Being Humble Is Having a Grounded View of Yourself

Meeting others as a brother or sister requires you to have a grounded view of yourself. In fact, the Latin root of humility, *humilis*, implies lowliness, literally *on the ground*, ***humus***. You don't necessarily consider yourself lowly, but you are in touch with the reality of who you are in the grand scheme of things. Yes, you feel good, and yes, you shine. You are not such a big deal however. Part of that is being grateful for all the gifts in your life as we discussed above, but it goes beyond that. It means recognizing that you are far from perfect. You're not Mary Poppins—"practically perfect in every way." That realization adjusts your attitude and your behavior.

> With a grounded view of yourself, you know that you have a lot to learn. You are a lifelong learner.

With a grounded view of yourself, you know that you have a lot to learn. You might know a lot, but you don't know it all. You are not puffed up. You aren't complacent with your understanding of yourself and your world. Others know more than you about many things and you want to learn from them. You are a lifelong learner. You engage with others with curiosity. You listen. You don't assume that you know better about things. Even in being generous, when you see someone's need, you don't assume that you know what is best to do for them or that you are more capable of fixing their situation or addressing their need than they are.

You accept criticism and don't let it make you wither. You want to improve because you, like everyone, are flawed—wonderfully, uniquely flawed in fact. So it is okay when you get feedback on how you might improve. You check your work and do a job thoroughly. You acknowledge your failures and weaknesses. You ask for forgiveness. That doesn't mean you go around saying you're sorry all of the time. That is often dishonest, and you want to be clear so dishonest apologies are something you reject. "I'm sorry" are precious words. You do not utter them in a reflexive, willy-nilly way. You do not utter them from a stance of arrogance. *If you say, "I'm sorry," then you really mean that you won't do it again and that if you could turn back the clock you wouldn't have done it in the first place.* If you can't or don't want to say that then you just ask sincerely, "Can you forgive me?" and you engage in dialogue about your failure with the other person. You don't blame others for your failures because you know that even if they contributed to a failure or problem, you did too.

You also know that others have gifts and talents that you don't have. You have the capacity to admire others, not just seek their admiration of you. You are good, but you don't make a big deal about it because others are good too. No matter what the field of human endeavor, there is always someone better. Talents and capacities to perform ebb and flow and there is always someone who is the next big thing. That doesn't make you depressed, jealous, and frustrated because it is just a reality that you accept.

You also know that you can't do it all. You need others. You ask for help. You ask for prayers. You offer help and prayer, well wishes and positive intention to others. They need help too. Why doesn't the proverbial man-in-charge want to ask for help? It's his pride, being afraid to admit to another that he is lost, afraid to appear weak and stupid. Being humble means you know that sometimes you are indeed weak and stupid in the sense that you don't have the ability to take care of things yourself and you don't know how to take care of things yourself. You can't do it alone. So you ask for help.

That doesn't mean that you view yourself as helpless. You are very capable and you do your best. *Quality is important to you.* You do your best not because you want to gain recognition and rewards. Those serve only your ego and when they come you receive them as gifts. You strive for excellence because that is the natural way for you to be. When you do something, you want to do it well. You want to create beauty and goodness because it brings you joy and it brings joy to others, not because it elevates you above others.

The challenge comes when you achieve success. You begin to think pretty highly of yourself. You start to project into the future and think of all that you could be and should be. This future oriented thinking is a delusion that takes you away from the moment, the now. You begin to make big plans for yourself. Your ambitions take over. You think about all that you can gain in fame and fortune. Suddenly, others become your means to achieve those expectations. Suddenly, when you create, you claim credit for the creation. When you interact with others, you look to control and use them to serve your goals. Your head has swollen. Your hat size is no longer in the one-size-fits-all range.

Being humble means that you have a grounded view of your success. Yes, it has to do with you and your efforts and talents. But it also has to do with luck and timing and gifts from God

> Being humble means that you have a grounded view of your success. Yes, it has to do with you and your efforts and talents. But it also has to do with luck and timing and gifts from God and others.

and others. Many, many others have contributed to your success—your parents, mentors, colleagues, competitors, friends, family, and everyone who is part of the web of community that you live in. In many ways, your success might just be an accident of fate. Maybe, maybe not, but being humble means you know it is never completely of your own making.

Being Humble Is Pitching In

When you are grateful for the gifts in your life, when you meet others as brothers and sisters, when you have a grounded view of yourself, you will be motivated to *act*—for yourself and for others.

> Action in humility involves service. You want to contribute to the common good because you see yourself as a part of something larger.

Action in humility involves service. You want to contribute to the common good because you see yourself as a part of something larger. Being humble means seeking first to serve rather than be served. It finds greatness in sacrifice and effort without the need for recognition. All around you there are opportunities for service, opportunities you might have passed up in the past.

Why didn't you serve? *Because you didn't have to*. It was the easiest thing to do. You were a ***free rider***. A free rider enjoys benefits without contributing—someone who rides the bus without paying the fare. It is an economic concept that has been proven to affect individual decision-making with regard to cooperating—or not. Anytime responsibilities or resources are shared, there are opportunities for free riders. A free rider is the roommate who never does the dishes, or who drinks all the beer in the fridge and never buys any. A free rider is the person who walks his dog in the park everyday and never cleans up the poop. A free rider lets the alley behind his house get overrun with trash and weeds. A free rider drives aggressively, runs a red light and parks his Mercedes between two spaces in the parking lot to make sure it won't get hit. On a larger scale, the free rider is the nation that over-fishes the seas and endangers the supply of fish for everyone, or a nation that enjoys the benefit of global security through its reliance on the power and resources of other nations. If a responsibility belongs to a group, then it's easy for some members of the group to do nothing. If a resource is freely shared in a group, it's easy for some members of the group to take more than their share. If a rule exists for the general good of all then it's easy for a few to ignore it.

Being a free rider is another form of pride, *placing yourself in a special category* where you deserve special treatment. You don't need to contribute or help out because someone else will and you can get away with it. You don't need to follow the same rules as others because there is no harm done if only one or two don't comply. As we discussed in connection with being clear, you can be dishonest because you trade on the fact that most people are honest.

You might say, "Free rider problems—yes, that's why we have laws and government and taxes." You would be right. Societies can organize and use laws and law enforcement resources to compel members to participate in doing collective good. Governments can tax citizens and use taxes to pay workers to take care of common responsibilities, to pay for law enforcement and to pay those who regulate citizens' use of common resources. But using law to govern behavior, to make sure everyone contributes, is very difficult. Laws have to be agreed upon in order to be enacted, and then government resources have to be allocated to enforcement of those laws. Often either or both of these are too insurmountable and as a result, free rider problems are everywhere. Communities simply can't use laws to compel people to do good. If those who don't comply or contribute are not likely to face negative consequences, then many are likely to neither comply nor contribute.

In a wealthy society, it is easy for free riders to take advantage of the good will of others. A free rider doesn't bring a food dish to a pot luck meal or the school class party because "It won't be noticed; there will be enough from everyone else." So, in an anonymous, transactional world, it is easy for free riders to take advantage of the good will of others. Being relational means you aren't anonymous and *you aren't a free rider.* Instead you are someone who recognizes situations where opportunities exist to be a free rider and you *choose* not to take advantage of the good will of others. You *choose* to contribute to the common good. With generosity, you choose to pay more, to do more, than what might be considered your ***fair share***. You pitch in. You volunteer. You do your part. You pay your taxes, but you don't just assume that, because you pay taxes, you have done all that you need to do.

We're not saying, "Get out there and take it upon yourself to fill in potholes on the county road." That would call too much attention to yourself, wouldn't it? Maybe, maybe not. You just do more, you give more—cheerfully. You choose to take the time to sort and donate gently used goods rather than pitching them in the trash. You know that what you do for the common good, for the good of yourself and others, makes your community, your world, a better place.

You know that what you do for the common good, for the good of yourself and others, makes your community, your world, a better place.

Being Humble Is Being Quiet and Lifting Up Others

Come back to where we started in looking at humility—your motivation. Your motivation drives your actions. When you pitch in, are you motivated by a desire to respect others and care about them? When humility is the foundation of your motivation, the way you are, both alone and among others, is different than the way you would be if your motivations were self-promotion, gaining attention and recognition, or winning. You are quiet.

What is being quiet? You are thoughtful, calm, maybe even shy or reserved. Maybe not. Being quiet does not mean you are invisible. Yet, you are not noisy, both in the sense of not vocally loud and forceful, but also in the sense of *not making a big effort to draw attention to yourself.* You don't spend a lot of time talking about yourself. You never boast. You are good, but you're not going to make a big deal about it. We are not saying that everyone should just wear a grey jumpsuit and surrender their individuality, but you also don't express yourself routinely, vocally or otherwise, in a way that shouts, "Look at me!"

"But hold on," you might say, "I care about my appearance and what people think of me. I take care of myself and I want to make a good impression." Yes, it is healthy to take care of yourself and care about how you look. That is modesty and positive self-regard. You can be both a part of the community and also be an individual. You might paint your face and put on a crazy hat when you go to see your favorite team and cheer them on heartily, you might sing loud and dance hard at your friend's wedding, you might have your hair and nails done and put on your best suit for a public appearance—you express yourself, but you are an individual whose individuality is expressed *in context* with others.

Being quiet also doesn't mean that you are not active. You have energy, but it is not frenetic. You are determined and willing to work hard—*alongside others*. Your desire is for group success, the group that you are part of—your family, your team, your company, your community, your nation, your planet. You are open to working for the betterment of something greater than yourself.

In humility, your means of achieving group success, for yourself and for others, is not through elevating yourself to power and prestige, but through *elevating the group by elevating its members*. Being quiet is part of that. You ask about others—not just a routine, "How are you doing?" but, "How are you doing, really?" from the heart, looking them in the eye. Then you listen without advising, interrupting, stealing their story, and without aligning and triangling. You give them space to speak and respect their ideas even if they aren't expressed forcefully. You encourage them. You make them feel important—meet them as brothers and sisters as we discussed earlier. You

> Being humble, being relational, means you lift up others, knowing that when you do, you are part of transformation, lasting positive change.

inspire their belief in themselves by your belief in their capacity to make a positive difference. You challenge them to go ahead and make it. Being humble, being relational, means you lift up others, knowing that when you do, you are part of transformation, lasting positive change. You empower others and use your power wisely in relation to them, which leads us to our final way of being relational—being kind.

Questions for Your Consideration

In exploring Being Humble, consider the following questions. If you are not sure about your answers, go back and visit the chapter.

- How do you balance your ego with humility?
- When you meet another person, do you typically place yourself above them (in command), below them (in deference), or do you do something else?
- What is the difference between seeing others as your "equals" versus seeing them as your "brothers or sisters"?
- When do you think that you deserve to be treated differently than others?
- What do you do when you receive criticism?
- What is your approach to stewardship for shared resources and responsibilities?

- In what ways do the contributions of prior generations make your life better?
- What is your definition of false humility?
- What do you mean when you say, "I'm sorry?"
- How is success challenging to your humility?

ORANS

Chapter Nine

Being Kind

Being kind might not seem so difficult when you think about it casually, but when you ***look harder*** at it, as you know to do in being grounded, you see that challenges to your kindness present themselves to you daily. It's easy to underestimate how challenging it is to be kind partly because kindness is not very clearly defined. It is often discussed very broadly and mixed with other qualities such as generosity and humility. It is considered kind to be generous, but giving to others is not the essence of kindness if it is to be considered separate and distinct from generosity. Kind and generous are not synonymous. Similarly, it is considered kind to act with humility, not placing yourself over, above, or in front of others, but, while humility might be essential to being kind, there is more to being kind than just being humble.

Being kind also is associated with a quality that is even more vague, being ***nice***. Are they the same? Maybe, maybe not. Kind certainly seems to have more gravitas. Maybe it's just a more adult version of nice. Most would say there are differences, but everyone seems to be able to agree that if you are ***mean*** then you are neither nice nor kind. So they do have in common, like other aspects of being relational, the characteristic that it is easier to define what the quality **is,** by stating what it is **not**.

You are *not* kind when:

- You use force to get your way.
- You respond to force with force.
- You lie to get what you want.
- You respond to lies with lies.
- You let anger drive your desire to harm another and you act on it.
- You beat the crap out of someone, anyone, literally or figuratively—even in something that is *just a game.*
- You twist someone's arm to get them to go along with you.
- You use fear and threats of punishment or harm to motivate others to follow or obey you.
- You punish others long and hard, so they learn a lesson when they do wrong.
- You roll over the interests of others because there isn't time to deal with them.
- You ignore the suffering or needs of others because you are not responsible for them.
- You do something, or neglect to do something, in order to get back at another person.
- You are passive aggressive saying yes and doing nothing because you didn't want to or didn't feel like it.

- You further the suffering of others by taking advantage of their weakness.
- You further the suffering of others by enabling it actively or even passively.
- You run away from trouble with another or quit when trouble becomes *not worth it.*

Perhaps we are just splitting hairs in defining kindness, but we want to get to the root of what it is to be kind and to offer you a clear vision of how you can meet the challenge of being kind so that you can be a force for lasting positive ***change***, and therefore be a relational leader.

At its core, being kind is about your **power** and how you use it.

At its core, being kind is about your **power** and how you use it.

Look Harder at Your Power

Everyone has power. As a winner you have lots of power. You may not realize all of the power that you have because you take it for granted and often you don't choose to use it. But let's hold off on looking at why you might not use your power and instead first ***look harder*** at your power and its sources.

The sources of your power are referred to as ***currencies***.[18] Like economic currencies—money—your power currencies increase, decrease, and flow between you and others. As with economic currency, your power currencies are spent and gained according to some value placed on them by others. Your power in relation

18 See Wilmot, William and Hocker, Joyce, *Interpersonal Conflict*, 7th Ed. (New York, 2007).

to another person depends on what they need or want from you and the value they place on that need or want. Without getting too abstract here, the point is that if nothing you are, if nothing you can do, if nothing you have the potential to be or do, has ***value*** to another person, then you have *no* ***power*** *in relation to* them. From this perspective, you might think that you have little power in many relationships or little power in many interactions. But you would be wrong—because you are not consciously aware of all of the power you have. Everyone has multiple sources of power, in varying amounts, in relation to other people. This is a premise of Transformative Conflict Theory. The first step in understanding what it means to be kind is to understand clearly your power in relation to another person and their power in relation to you.

The first step in understanding what it means to be kind is to understand clearly your power in relation to another person and their power in relation to you.

Here's a baker's dozen of power currencies:

First, you have **physical power**. This is the most basic form of your power. It's about size and strength. You use your body and extensions of it—such as tools and weapons—to affect others positively or negatively. Maybe you can knock someone down, hit them, or throw a rock at them. Or maybe you can extend your hand to help someone up, or use your hands and skills to fix something or feed someone. You, in a car, can run someone over or give them a ride. You, with a gun in your hand, can shoot someone down or lay your gun down. The other with a gun in their hand can shoot you down or lay their gun down. You can overpower them or you can collapse. You can walk up to someone who has a gun in their hand and stand before them defenseless. How do you use your personal physical power? How do others use their personal physical power in relation to you? Physical power is also about how companies, organizations, and governments use ***muscle*** to advance their interests—boots on the ground, weapons of all kinds. How do you use your physical power then? How do others use their physical power in relation to you?

You have **sexual power**. You are attractive. You are desirable. Others want to be with you sexually, or maybe they just want to be around you because your desirability will enhance theirs. You can use your sexuality to give pleasure, show love, create unity, and potentially make new life. Others want those things from you and you know that. You can use your sexuality or withhold it—to influence someone or get money or satisfaction and other things valuable to you. How do you use your sexual power? How do others use sexual power in relation to you?

You have **emotional power**. Your emotions affect others. Your anger intimidates. Your happiness radiates. Your anxiety makes others anxious. Your suspicion and mistrust breeds the same in others. When you feel embarrassed, ashamed, powerless, confused, victimized, betrayed, sad, guilty, depressed, disgusted, or offended—to name just a few powerful emotions—others get sucked into your emotional state. When you feel joyful, euphoric, secure, content, satisfied, confident, cheerful, relaxed, hopeful, or energized—or all these things at once (maybe, maybe not!)—others are elevated by your mood. You may or may not be able to control your emotions, but your thinking and how you focus your attention has a lot to do with that control, and if you are grounded and centered, you can use your emotional power positively—or not. It's your choice. How does your emotional power affect others? How does theirs affect you?

You have **spiritual power**. There is power in your mere presence. Who you are as a being projects power. Your heart and mind and soul are felt by others and affect them. Your intentions, held in the secrecy of your heart, or shared only in your private thoughts and prayers, affect those around you. You don't have to do or say anything to have power. You have it by your very presence. Others can feel your essence and know its value. Hold a baby in your arms and you know its spiritual power as a totally vulnerable, dependent creature, yet one for whom you would make great sacrifices. Others know when they wound you and when they bring joy to your spirit. They crave a spiritual connection. You can use your spiritual power to wound or bring joy to others. You can put your spiritual power on the shelf, bury it in worldly concerns, and withhold your spirit from others who need and want your presence or you can wake up, show up, and let others feel the difference your presence makes. How do you use your spiritual power? How do others use their spiritual power in relation to you?

You have **relationship power**. You're popular. You know people. They like you and you have built their loyalty to you. You have contacts, social currency. You have circles of influence. Others look to you to help them gain credibility with and acceptance by the people you know. Others want to be with you in order to be more popular, accepted, and trusted. You can use your relationship power to help others join a group that you are part of or you can use it to exclude someone from the group. You can use your relationship power to build bridges between groups of people or drive them apart. You can use your relationship power in destructive triangling or in unitive triangling. How do you use your relationship power? How do others use relationship power in relation to you?

You have **cooperative power**. You have free will. You can go along with others or not. You can support an idea or not. You can cooperate with authority or not. You can follow the law or not. Others want you to cooperate with them. They don't want you to resist or refuse to comply. You can use your cooperative power to support something. You can refuse to cooperate and use that power to undermine support for something. How do you use your cooperative power? How do others use cooperative power in relation to you?

You have **communicative power**. You speak well. You write well. You have a command of language. You are aware of your voice and you use it. Your voice is clear and strong. You can express your thoughts clearly. You have a good sense of humor and can make people laugh. Maybe you can speak several languages. You can think on your feet and respond quickly. You are engaged. You can patiently listen to others and help them express their thoughts clearly. You can ask questions to get a clear understanding. Your communication skills give you power in many situations, and others respect that power and want you to use it to help them. You can use words to persuade others, help them see different perspectives, and appreciate complexity in situations that they might not have seen. You use words to show others love, care, and compassion. You can use words to entertain, inform, and amuse others. You also use your communicative power to nag and complain, deceive others, provide them bad information, verbally abuse and belittle them, or incite their anger. You can use your communicative power, along with emotional power, to incite and inflame others or assure and inspire them. How do you use your communicative power? How do others use communicative power in relation to you?

You have **broadcast power**. Building on communicative power, you may have the ability to get your messages out to a great number of people. You have a lot of followers on Facebook, Twitter, Instagram, and YouTube. You may be a regular on television or radio. You may be a newspaper columnist or reporter. You may be the owner of a media company. You may have a lot of readers of your blog or just be a person who regularly puts your opinions out there through comments on what others write. You are a regular contributor to Amazon and eBay ratings. Others want you to use your broadcasting to help them. You can use your broadcast power to amplify the positive or negative aspects of your communicative power. How do you use your broadcast power? How do others use their broadcast power in relation to you?

You have **knowledge power**. You have expertise that another person values and can't easily get from another source. You know something that another person does not know that might be important to them. You have experience that has taught you valuable lessons. You have spent 10,000 hours becoming a master in something. You can use your knowledge to make a living and serve others or you can use it to exploit their lack of knowledge to your advantage. You can withhold your knowledge or give it freely. How do you use your knowledge power? How do others use knowledge power in relation to you?

You have **talent power**. You can do something exceptionally well. You do it in a way others can't. You do it with a certain style that others like. Whether or not you have spent 10,000 hours honing your skill, your talent is organic, it is yours alone. It is a gift you have as part of your DNA that no matter how much effort others may exert to be like you or to do what you do, your talent is unique to you. Others want you to use your talent in some way that serves them—for entertainment, economically or otherwise. Others want to be around you because they admire your talent. They may want to be close to the positive attention that your talent attracts. You can use your talent to make a living—or maybe even get rich. You can use it to build your personal celebrity status. You can use your talent to create, pursue excellence, and enrich your life and the lives of others. You can use the attention that your talent attracts, with its attendant broadcast power, to promote yourself or to support a worthy cause and inspire others. How do you use your talent power? How do others use talent power in relation to you?

You have **economic power**. You have control over economic resources that others want. You have access to and authority over resources of time, finances, services, and raw goods. You have money to spend, you have money to save, you have money to invest, and you have money to give away. You have the ability to decide who gets paid and how much they get paid. You can decide which projects, causes, or organizations are supported and which ones are not supported. Your economic power influences others' economic futures. Others want you to use your economic power in ways that benefit them or that support organizations they have an interest in. You can use your economic power to gain more economic power. You can use it to maximize your benefit in any transaction. You can use economic power to enrich or to exploit. You can be generous, or not. How do you use your economic power? How do others use economic power in relation to you?

You have **positional power**. You are part of some larger entity—your family, community, company, nation, or club, including your pinochle club—that has vested you with some authority over others and control over resources or systems. You're a boss in some way, shape, or form. You have positional power because *you* chose it: You are a parent. You have positional power because someone chose it *for you*: You have been elected or appointed to lead others. You have created a business that employs others. They want you to use your authority—and its attendant power to control rewards, gifts, punishments, penalties, preferences, and prices—to benefit, or at least not harm, them. You can use your positional power to oppress others, keep them down. You can use your positional power to gain more power and serve your ambition to climb to a position of higher authority. You can wield your positional authority like a whip and motivate others with fear. You can hold a position and enjoy its benefits while doing the minimum to get by and protecting your backside. You can use your position to inspire, motivate, care for, and lift up others. You can disempower others or you can empower others. You can turn a blind eye to your rank and plunge forward until your time is up, or you can consider the future of others with thoughtful succession plans. You can use your position to seize immediate gain and attention for yourself or build lasting value that will serve others for many years to come. How do you use your positional power? How do others use positional power in relation to you?

You have **temporal power**. Your attitudes about time, your perceptions of the pressures of time, and its scarcity in relation to all of the things you want to happen or get done, affect others. Others want you to give your time to them and to their needs and demands. They want you to respect their deadlines and their urgency. You can do something now or you can put it off until later. You can slow down a difficult conversation or you can speed it up. You can be early, on time, late, or absent for work, for appointments, and for meetings. You can let time constraints create great anxiety or you can let things happen at their own pace. You can be driven by artificial deadlines or you can create realistic deadlines. You can adhere to reasonable deadlines or you can let them pass. You can avoid doing something because you don't have the time, or you can stop and make time. How do you use your temporal power? How do others use temporal power in relation to you?

That's a lot of power. There are more sources, but we hope you will think this is a pretty good power inventory, our ***baker's dozen*** for you to consider. Look at power currencies closely in connection with relationships where you believe you have a great deal of power and those where you think you don't have much. Understanding your sources of power helps you identify your options—paths of action you can choose. Having options gives you power in your dealings with others, but you have no power unless you are aware of your options. Chances are you have more power than you think in many situations where you assume you have little or no power. Chances also are that in relationships where you think you have a great deal of power, others have more power than you think they do. Winners like you have many power currencies to draw upon.

Understanding your sources of power helps you identify your options. Having options gives you power in your dealings with others

For each source of power, we ask, "*How do you use it?*" because every power currency can be used to be relational or in ways that are purely transactional. Every form of power can be used in ways that are kind and in ways that are unkind. You can also be kind or unkind in the ways you choose *not* to use your power, positively in exercising restraint or forbearance, or negatively through indifference or neglect. Let's take a look at kindness and how you use your power.

Every form of power can be used in ways that are kind and in ways that are unkind.

Being Kind Is Respecting Self-Determination

We have a fundamental tenet in our work as mediators, to respect self-determination. That means that we *do not try to force any decision* on another person, even if we think it is in their best interest, and, with very limited exceptions related to safety, we do not try to "get" someone to *do* or *not do* anything. Our role as mediators gives us special insight into the power of respect for self-determination in achieving lasting and satisfying outcomes to conflict situations. When you are acting as a neutral in any conflict between others, promoting others' self-determination is usually a very helpful frame for your role, however in situations where you have a stake in the matter, where you *do* want to get somebody to do or not do something, you might want to toss the idea of respect for self-determination out the window.

We would urge you not to. Respecting others' self-determination in many ways is the essence of kindness. You can use your power to force others, against their will, to do what you wish, but it is unkind to do so. It is also unwise. What is your reaction when you are forced to do something against your will? Resentment? Blaming? Maybe even desire for revenge. And so it is

Force or coercion of any kind, fuels a cycle of conflict. Perhaps not immediately, but definitely in time.

with others. Force or coercion of any kind, fuels a cycle of conflict. Perhaps not immediately, but definitely in time. It sows the seeds of discontent. It is bad karma. In truth, it is a failure on your part to use all your non-coercive power to persuade the person to make a different decision.

We know this well as mediators. In that role, we are proactive about process, which means we safeguard our clients' self-determination. Mediators, guided by the Transformative Theory of Conflict, believe deeply that people, even in conflict, have what it takes to be both strong and responsive to the other, for when doing so, a new opening is created for what is possible.

Mediators, guided by the Transformative Theory of Conflict, believe deeply that people, even in conflict, have what it takes to be both strong and responsive to the other, for when doing so, a new opening is created for what is possible.

When people are given the opportunity to engage in meaningful ways fostered by the mediator's presence and relational interventions, amazing things happen. The mediator doesn't have to *get* or *force* people to do anything. Their own clarity will emerge and their experience of empowerment will pave the way forward for better interactions and more informed decisions that are natural byproducts of this kind of dialogue—the kind of dialogue that happens when people are given the chance to engage in centered, grounded, and clear ways. A mediator's continued belief in others' self-determination is an act of kindness since a mediator must constantly exercise forbearance and neither shut down nor get in the way of meaningful interaction. You, as winners, potential relational leaders, are what we like to call "little m" mediators all the time. While you are not invested with the professional ethical standards and indeed you may have a stake in the outcome yourself, you too can foster quality interaction. When people are given the chance and encouragement to interact in relational ways, from a place of personal strength and connection to others, whether they agree or disagree, they have a much better chance of being open and kind.

So, respecting self-determination means that you let the other decide what to do and you do not use force to get them to do your will. What does that mean? Let's start with **violence**. We will talk about self-defense later, but using physical force that can harm another person is not kind, is it?

Similarly—***threats*** of violence—*not kind.*

Coercion through deception, discussed above in being clear—*not kind.*

Coercion through the use of any of the baker's dozen types of power discussed above—*not kind.*

You can probably think of many examples of how the abuse of power through coercion takes place, but for the sake of illustration, consider the classic ***bully.***

We will refer to the bully as just that. However, let us say that we hold the belief that people who use bullying tactics do not at their core want to be bullies. Bullying actions are often learned or are defense responses to a past where they themselves were or felt bullied. For the sake of shorthand, we will refer to those who engage in bullying tactics as bullies, but we hold the belief that they are more than their bullying behavior and we do not want to label them as bullies. We will focus on the type of behavior they trade on and ways to be relational.

The bully—male or female—uses physical power to harm and harass; uses emotional power to intimidate and create fear; uses sexual power to extort; uses communicative power to demean and belittle; uses broadcast power to spread false rumors and insults; uses relationship power to demonize and exclude; uses economic power to oppress and squeeze the last dollar out of a deal; uses temporal power to create stress and anxiety; uses positional power to stonewall, punish and control. The *bully's goal is domination, control of others, avoiding responsibility for wrongdoing or failures, and gaining resources* such as special treatment or money.

The institutional bully also uses size to harm and harass. Taking advantage of the weakness of others, putting out slanted truths, covering up their weaknesses as they exploit others. The goal is the same: power over others.

As a winner, you have many opportunities to be the bully. Being kind means *you are not the bully*. But it also means that you don't respond to the bully by using power in any of the ways the bully uses power. As a winner you might not have been bullied. The bully didn't bother with you, they found easier, weaker targets. Maybe, maybe not. But how you respond to a bully is essential to being relational.

How you respond to a bully is essential to being relational.

Being Kind Is Being Strong and Brave

So how does kindness respond to the bully? *With kindness.* But that's not weakness or cowardice. Rather it is kindness in strength and with courage. You don't ignore the conflict; you engage with it. You engage with dialogue, not with violence or coercive power. You stay centered, grounded, and clear. You seek to *persuade*, but you respect the bully's self-determination. You seek change through conversion, not coercion.[19]

You are brave because you are **vulnerable**. You are strong enough to be vulnerable. Which is more brave? Stopping a bully by beating them up, or facing a bully without resorting to violence? Being kind means you expose yourself to possible harm—be it physical, emotional, economic, reputational, temporal, and so on. You take the risk. You refuse to use the ways of the bully in response to the bully. You also don't run away from conflict with a bully unless it is just to buy some time, to retreat temporarily, in order to organize, consider your options, and find your sources of power. You don't passively submit to the bully.

The classic advice is to *stand up* to a bully. Being relational means you don't stand up to a bully by returning the bully's violence with violence, intimidation with intimidation, lies with lies. You *sit down* with a bully—if possible. If need be, you *wear them out* with dialogue—relentless engagement. When you are afraid or angry, that might be the hardest and bravest thing you ever do.

You are strong because you *know* that, even in your vulnerability and refusal to use coercion, you have many other sources of power. Being kind in response to the bully does not mean you don't use your power. In fact you might need to use all your power currencies more fully than you ever have. Let's look at how you do that.

---

19 See Gandhi, Mahatma, *The Essential Gandhi*, L. Fisher Ed. (New York, 2002).

Self Defense—
There's No Such Thing as "Just War"

You might be saying, "Kindness is good when you are dealing with reasonable people, even if they are bullies, but what about when you or those you care for are in real ***danger***? Isn't force used in self-defense or in defense of innocent others okay?" Legally—Yes. Morally, in many faith traditions—Yes. But the real answer if you are being relational is—**No**. Why? Because you have *options* and you have many more sources of power. You don't *need* to use force. If you are not absolutely required to use force, it is unacceptable to use force. The challenge is to use our intelligence, creativity and imagination to conceive the means to defend against aggression without resorting to coercion.

The challenge is to use our intelligence, creativity and imagination to conceive the means to defend against aggression without resorting to coercion.

We hear all the time in our mediation work praise and support from many who speak about how important dialogue and engagement is—for **other** people. But when those same folks experience their **own** conflicts, they will often change their minds and say, "Dialogue is good in all those other situations, but not this one; the other person is impossible." Or, if they are attorneys, they may say "Mediation is all fine for everybody else's cases, but not mine; I deal with crazy people or people on the other side who are totally unreasonable." Just because the other is viewed as unreasonable or impossible, the quickly-decided shift is to litigation—a civil form of war—often won by the winners—those with the most resources and ability to wage the battle. War is abandoning kindness in favor of coercive power-based solutions.

In justifying the use of military force there is the concept of ***Just War***. There are different versions of its formulation, but all basically provide conditions under which it is considered just and morally acceptable to go to war and use military force against an enemy. It might seem like we are getting far afield from our discussion of being kind here, but we would ask you to hang with us as we try to make a point about kindness, the use of force, and self-defense.

Under Just War doctrine, as with any definition of the circumstances where force is considered justified in response to aggression, in self-defense or in defense of others, a person (or nation) using force must conclude that *all other means* of responding to the aggression are "*impractical or ineffective*."[20] It is the idea that war should be a *last resort*. The same goes with any use of force. Being relational, being kind, means you take that very seriously and you *use every bit of your wit and energy and power to meet conflict with kindness and make the conscious decision not to use force and coercion*. If you do make such a conscious decision, you will find many other ways to persuade, convert, and achieve your goals of lasting positive change. So, in reality, in our world today, there is no such thing as Just War.

There are well known examples in history for you to draw upon—the struggle for independence in India led by Mahatma Gandhi, the civil rights movement in the United States led by Rev. Martin Luther King, Jr. How did Gandhi and King and the millions

---

20 See Catechism of the Catholic Church ¶ 2309.

of people who joined them creatively use their power currencies? Today there are millions of people engaged in nonviolent efforts to bring about lasting positive change. Witness the work of the Nonviolent Peaceforce, a group which sends unarmed civilians into foreign conflicts to foster dialogue and provide a protective presence for threatened civilians.[21] It is work. It takes great commitment, but they are making a difference in places where conflict is chronic like South Sudan and Myanmar. They are reducing fear and giving confidence to threatened people who find themselves living in harm's way. We would say they are advocates intentionally being relational, even in the face of grave danger.

In thinking about efforts to resolve conflict without resort to violence and coercion, the first thing that comes to mind is *diplomacy and negotiation*. Yes, negotiation is at the heart of a response that respects self-determination, but it is negotiation in a very broad sense, *not just formal talks* that might ***break down*** and ***fail*** thus justifying resort to the use of force because all other means are ***impractical or ineffective***.

Negotiation with an aggressor, in the broad sense, would include many possible uses of power. Let's look again at our baker's dozen through an individual lens, looking at what you might personally, individually do, but *asking you to also consider how such individual action might also be representative of and analogous to actions possibly taken by groups of people organized into political parties, corporations, or nation states.*

---

21 See *www.NonviolentPeaceforce.org.*

Using Your Power with Kindness

> In responding to bullying or to others using coercive power against you, you can employ other power currencies. You have options in responding with kindness.

In responding to bullying or to others using coercive power against you, you can employ other power currencies. You have options in responding with kindness. Lots of them.

You could increase your physical power. Get stronger physically? Work out? Maybe, maybe not an option for you. You could get a weapon even though you have no intention of using it. "Speak softly and carry a big stick," as Teddy Roosevelt famously preached. You have heard it said that if you are armed and dangerous no one will mess with you. Maybe, maybe not. That might be true, but isn't that just using a form of coercion—the threat of violence? Besides, you might just set off an arms race of sorts—escalating power and threats, raising the stakes of the conflict. Ultimately, *increasing your physical power puts you in great risk of having to use it.* How will you justify having invested so much in being stronger if you won't use your strength? But you know your use of physical power will only inflame the bully's desire for revenge—even if you are perfectly justified. Maybe the bully will leave you alone, but maybe not. Maybe they will just go pick on someone else. You don't want that, do you? Maybe it sounds good in the short run, but what about the longer run? You don't know when they might choose an opportune moment for retaliation. Sounds like a focus on increasing your physical power might be a bad option, right?

You could use your sexual power to seduce the aggressor, merge with them, and try to make their desire for you overcome their aggression or resistance to your persuasion. But that would force you to compromise yourself in ways that are completely unacceptable to you, right? You risk great harm to your spirit and sense of integrity. You would be in bed with a bully. This is not being kind to yourself. Another bad option.

Look hard at your emotional power. Don't hide it. What you feel is important. Being strong enough to be vulnerable means that you are not afraid to show your emotions. The actions of the bully hurt you, may make you sad, angry, afraid, and frustrated. You feel pain. Show these emotions to the bully. Express these emotions. Use words. Your authentic tears are okay. Projecting your emotions through physical power is not. Let the bully feel what you feel. It might touch their interior sense of decency and compassion. It might not. They might feel some shame in ways you will never know. They might not. But you have nothing to lose and you both have everything to gain relationally. Having emotions is not weakness. It is human. We have been given a full spectrum of emotions as part of our humanity. Experience them and articulate them. Even anger can be relational if channeled in a centered and grounded way. If all you do is put on the brave, strong face, do you show the bully that they have harmed a real person with a soul? A person who might be their brother or sister?

Having emotions is not weakness. It is human.

Look hard at your spiritual power. You remain optimistic in adversity. You are sober about the situation, you are grounded in reality, yet your hope never wavers. You let the bully know that they can hurt you, but they can't take away your dignity. You stay solid in your sense of yourself as a person worthy of respect. You stay centered in your belief in a better future. You are clear about bringing good intentions for the bully in your thoughts. You pray for the bully. You pray for yourself. You pray for wise and compassionate interactions, actions, and reactions in relation to the bully. You stand firm in your faith that your kindness will not be in vain. You believe *good will always triumph* over evil in the end. Indeed, all evil is temporary. You engage. You express these truths to the bully.

Now you are feeling **stronger** aren't you?

Look hard at your relationship power. You use your connections with others and your cooperative power with them to let the bully know that *you don't stand alone*. You aren't triangling against the bully and demonizing them, but you do let the bully know that ultimately their actions will isolate and alienate them from relationship with many people. You build your coalition with integrity and truthfulness.

Look hard at your cooperative power. Your *nonviolent noncooperation*, as espoused by Gandhi, is powerful. It can take many forms in response to a bully. You don't play by their rules. You don't make it easy for them. You don't submit. You don't go along. You resist actively, but not with physical force. You withhold the power of your knowledge and talent from service to their goals. You organize a boycott. You won't pay their taxes. You won't be part of their system. You organize and cooperate with others to help you in your resistance. You get in the way of their efforts to achieve their goals. You might end up injured, in jail or worse, but you won't cooperate with the bully. You always hold open the invitation to dialogue. You are exhausting to deal with. There is

There is no honor or glory for the bully in crushing and defeating you if kindness is your response to bullying.

no honor or glory for the bully in crushing and defeating you if kindness is your response to bullying.

Look hard at your communicative and broadcast power. These are perhaps your greatest sources. You use them to persuade and engage the bully as much as possible—relentlessly. You use them to persuade and inform anyone who might support or enable the efforts of the bully. You know that bullies trade on weaknesses and false or hidden information. You communicate your emotions, your spiritual strength, your injuries, and the injustices you have suffered. You tell someone with authority over the bully. You file a formal complaint. You use words, images, music, video, whatever media you can get your hands on, to change hearts and minds in your favor. You use the biggest megaphone you can find to get your message out—television, Facebook, Twitter, whatever—but you do it with *integrity*. You remain centered, grounded, and clear. If you and the bully are both within an organization, you might need to be discreet and sensitive to the damage your communications might do to the organization. You are not waging a war of words. You are not demonizing the bully. Your goal in conflict is quality dialogue. If you file a formal complaint, you find the right advocate who understands your intentions to bring the bully to the dialogue table, for face-to-face interactions. Your intent is not to stir up litigation and use coercive threats. From quality dialogue, you believe that positive outcomes can emerge. You are always willing to sit down with the bully in a safe, confidential setting, with a mediator if possible—a mediator trained to respect fully rights to self-determination.

Look hard at your temporal power. Time is on your side. You can slow things down. The longer you persist in your efforts, the more likely the bully is to give up, realize the loneliness of the isolation their aggression has caused, or maybe have a change of heart. You just *don't give up* and you *don't give in*. You have staying power. You have perseverance to stick it out and continue to remain open, grounded in reality.

Sometimes, *in the moment, you may be forced to make a choice* to try to protect yourself or others from an aggressor—the *archetypical self-defense situation*. In these cases, time truly is not on your side at all. You might have to act in a split second. You might be able to run away. There is no shame in that if you are not abandoning others. In fact, it is the preferred course. It buys you time to marshal resources to deal with the aggressor. *But if harm to others is an immediate risk, you can stand and fight to protect them.*[22] There is no shame in that if your intentions are only to use as much force as needed to stop the immediate threat. Once the immediate threat is gone, your focus shifts to care for anyone wounded, even the aggressor. If you harm them, you will need to work to heal the wound you created. You don't want your injury of another to lead to their resentment and desire for revenge on you, or on the group you represent, in their eyes.

For winners, these situations are rare. We hope you are never in one. Slow things down if you can. Engage the aggressor in dialogue if you can. Kindness doesn't mean you just submit to harm,

---

22 We don't want to get too wrapped around the axle here in discussing self-defense, but we would acknowledge that there is a difference between standing and fighting in the moment when a threat to others emerges and you too are present versus going out of your way to swoop in and *intervene* physically and forcefully in a violent exchange between others to defend someone from the perceived "aggressor." The latter is much more problematic, for instance where force is used to intervene in a foreign civil war. In such situations, the course of kindness demands that all forms of power other than physical force be used to deal with the situation no matter how urgent. Intervention in urgent conflict between others might require urgent action, but violence would remain unnecessary just as it would in less urgent situations.

but in these emergent situations where you face grave harm, it might mean you surrender rather than fight. *Think about what the aggressor's goal is*—getting money or property? Inflicting harm or asserting power to serve some twisted criminal intent that is most likely a manifestation of some mental illness or injury? Having fully considered what it means to be kind in the face of aggression, think now about what you might do. It is up to you to judge the appropriate course.

> Being kind means you don't believe that alternatives to the use of force are impractical and ineffective.

In the end, being kind means you don't believe that alternatives to the use of force are impractical and ineffective. You have lots of power that is not coercive. You just have to have the will to use it. Resorting to violence and force is a *failure to use your imagination and creativity* to explore fully and be serious about using *alternative* sources of power.

Being relational calls you to do that and also calls you to use your power to influence the families, businesses, organizations, communities, states, and nations of which you are a part to follow the same course of kindness. It is the wise course. It is the course to lasting positive change. Being relational might mean you join a peace protest. Maybe, maybe not. It's your choice.

Being Kind Is Actively Caring— The Compassionate Impulse

Having looked at kindness in your interactions with those who have power over you (or at least they are *trying* to have power over you!)—the bullies—now let's turn our attention to how you use your power in relation to those over whom *you* have power and those you encounter whom you perceive as having less or equal power in relation to you. The bully is coming at you with aggression. Most people in your life aren't doing that. You meet them in many different postures: as equals, as people serving you, as anonymous people you encounter, as people presenting their needs to you. Being humble means that you meet them as a brother or sister—just like they were a member of your family. How do you treat someone as family? With kindness. That means you are *actively caring in relation to them.*

There are two parts to that—active and caring. Active means that when you encounter someone in need, you *do something.* Easy to say, hard to do. If you live in a large urban area, you encounter people in need all the time. The rational approach is to say, "I can't help everybody, so I will just go about my business and take care of my friends and family." This is the same dilemma you face in being generous. You might think your personal resources are scarce and you need to reserve and preserve them.

You don't. There is no limit to your kindness. You can be kind all day, every day, to everyone. That doesn't mean that you go around trying to rescue everyone and giving away all your resources. Although you might. You might see ten people in a day, you might see hundreds, but as you encounter someone, *you do something kind.* That could be as simple as a friendly look in the eye, a smile and hello. That could be a much more significant act of generosity. There are thousands of ways—check out *www.RandomActsofKindness.org.* You are not passive in your kindness. You're not a bystander. It's not just kind thoughts in your head and good intentions. When you feel a caring impulse toward another person, you act. You *don't do the sensible, reserved, thing*—just passing by, eyes set straight ahead, fixed on the horizon, not giving attention to what is happening right around you.

You might think, "I don't have the time for all that!" Yes, you do. Time pressure is the enemy of caring. Most of it is only in your mind. You stay grounded and try not to let your thoughts about time scarcity drive your actions. Indeed, sometimes it might take more time to be kind, but you think of all the good will that you are generating, the good karma that you are creating. You **believe** that there is always enough time to be kind and so there always is. Being kind means that time constraints are never your excuse not to be actively caring.

The second part of kindness when you are being relational is the *core—caring for others*. You are polite. You are considerate of others according to the sense of etiquette that you were raised in. But kindness is deeper. When you see suffering and pain, you feel compassion. You can empathize—connect with the emotional state of another. Brain science supports this phenomenon. When you are alert and awake and notice and enter into the same experience of another, mirror neurons fire in the brain. A flow of oxytocin brings a feeling of warmth in your body, your immediate experience of the other person's condition affects you, and you have the urge to be responsive.[23] You have a *compassionate impulse*.

Compassion is a complex emotion. Your capacity to feel it might not be well developed. As a winner, you might not have a lot of experience with pain and suffering—at least not on a deep level—to draw upon empathically. Maybe, maybe not. Recall our discussion

---

23 See Goleman, Daniel, *Social Intelligence* (New York, 2006).

of conflict transformation at the very beginning of this book. Conflict places you in a state of relative self-absorption in relation to another person. You may experience that as suspicion, defensiveness, being self-protective, or just being stuck in your narrow point of view, your own frame—unable to step into the perspective of another. Compassion is that emotion that allows you to shift from self-absorption to being attentive to the other person. That manifests as *more openness, willingness to accept the other's good faith and less concern about your vulnerability* in relation to them.

Compassion is that emotion that allows you to shift from self-absorption to being attentive to the other person.

You reflect back exactly what someone reports as their experience—using their words, not yours. It is an act of kindness when you choose to use your power to foster empowerment rather than to dominate or control. In the everyday moments of interaction, we can use our power so easily in ways that are not kind with the result that the opportunities presented for quality dialogue are stunted, stolen, diluted, or torn down. Being kind means you are willing to be vulnerable when you encounter others in pain or suffering, willing to risk rejection when you extend your kindness to them. You have the courage to be compassionate. You have the strength to find that courage.

In the everyday moments of interaction, we can use our power so easily in ways that are not kind with the result that the opportunities presented for quality dialogue are stunted, stolen, diluted, or torn down. Being kind means you are willing to be vulnerable when you encounter others in pain or suffering, willing to risk rejection when you extend your kindness to them.

You can develop that courage and increase your capacity to feel compassion. You are attentive to your *own* suffering and pain. You don't numb it out, run from it, or suppress it. Being grounded, you know that much of your suffering comes from your thoughts and your attachment to an idea about how things *should be* instead of how they are. You have learned to relax into that and to love the way things are, just as they *are*. You have learned to pay attention to where the attachment is lodged in your body and to be curious about it. You have learned to focus on resourcing a part of your body that is not caught up in the attachment or experience. You know that your suffering is temporary and will pass. But you are willing to attend to it in the now. Being in tune with your own suffering and how you cope with it will help you be in tune with the suffering of others. You will be primed to respond with compassion.

Being in tune with your own suffering and how you cope with it will help you be in tune with the suffering of others. You will be primed to respond with compassion.

How do you know it's compassion? Your body, your heart, your head give you cues. You feel welling within you the desire to be responsive to others with their suffering and you *think*, "How can I respond in a relational way?" or, if they are right there with you, you *ask*, "How can I help you?" You can't predict the response, but *you can make the offer*. Your offer matters. Then you prepare to make good on your offer—by being generous and by being patient, forgiving, and gentle.

While being relational embodies seven ways of being in our everyday lives and interactions, each of the seven ways needs the other ways, and all of the seven ways are interdependent on each other. To engage, you are centered and grounded and clear. To be clear, you need to be grounded in reality and truth. To be centered, you need to be clear about what is important to you. To be generous, you are clear about your power currencies. To be humble, you stay centered for authenticity. When you are relational, you use your power currencies in ways that are kind. You don't rob others of their means to engage meaningfully with others. You don't steal others' opportunities for empowerment and responsiveness. Being relational believes in amazing outcomes, ones you may not even imagine but that you know are possible, and you are patient.

While being relational embodies seven ways of being in our everyday lives and interactions, each of the seven ways needs the other ways, and all of the seven ways are interdependent on each other.

Being Kind Is Being Patient

Kindness has a lot to do with generosity. Acts of generosity, offered in humility, are invariably kind. We don't want to get too caught up in definitions; as we have seen, many of the ways of being relational blend and overlap. But, to us, being patient, forgiving, and gentle seem especially within the realm of being kind.

Again, kindness is about your power and how you use it.

Patience draws upon your humility and groundedness.

Patience draws upon your humility and groundedness. If you have a child you probably have developed patience. It is good to call upon your experience with children in cultivating your patience with others. Being kind means *you do not rush others*. Earlier we talked about time pressure as the enemy of caring. Being patient means that you don't let time pressure get the better of you especially when you are dealing with people over whom you have power. You might have the power to push and hurry them, but you don't. If there is something that is creating time pressure for you, you engage with the other person and let them know what is going on. You explain what is creating your urgency and you look harder at whether or not that urgency is real.

Often the urgency only exists in your *mind* because of something that you believe *must* happen within some time frame. You might be afraid of the consequences if the thing doesn't happen in the time you think it should. Are those consequences real or are you just assuming the worst? Maybe, maybe not. Are you concerned because a delay might cause you to have to re-think your plans or extend yourself and give more effort than you want to? Being patient means that you are *willing to accept inconveniences* for the sake of kindness to others.

Sometimes inconveniences come because of your failure to prepare and manage others and a situation. Pause. Being kind means relaxing and forgiving yourself. This almost immediately brings ease to an otherwise impatient situation. Sometimes inconveniences come to you because of something another person has done or failed to do. Maybe they were late, maybe they forgot, maybe they weren't paying attention or really even trying. Pause. When your patience is tested by the failures of others, being kind means being forgiving.

Being Kind Is Being Forgiving

How you respond to an injury or inconvenience is an important choice for you and for the other who injured you. Your response can set off a cycle of acrimony and revenge or start the process of healing and possibly lasting positive change. Forgiveness is at the heart of conflict transformation and quality dialogue is often the path to it. A common impulsive reaction when you are injured is to focus on your pain and become self-absorbed in a way that shuts down your ability to see the other as anything but "the offender who hurt me."

How you respond to an injury or inconvenience is an important choice for you and for the other who injured you.

Forgiveness is at the heart of conflict transformation and quality dialogue is often the path to it.

The degree to which you experience the injury might be related to a prior injury and the way that it was experienced and resolved, or not resolved. Regarding an injury that stuns you or stops you in your tracks, often it is because you have never experienced anything like it before and it throws you off center because you have no frame of reference. You might just move on. The memory you store about the event is one held more in the vein of wonder or curiosity than anything else. Or perhaps after a moment, you regain your center and let the other know how totally unexpected or surprised you are and ask if what you experienced is what they actually intended. They might be largely unaware of their impact on you.

On the other hand, the injury you find hard to shake might be related to a prior injury that was never fully attended to, never healed. When the new injury happens, it's as if an old scab is ripped off, as if the energy that went underground to be expended on tamping down, scabbing over, and forgetting the old injury is inflamed again. So your reaction can seem too big, out of proportion to what actually happened. You are having a conflict experience.

A common conflict reaction is to blame and heap on more, whether silently or noisily, out of revenge or in self-defense. Another common conflict reaction is to pretend everything's okay, escape, leave, get far away—whether mentally, emotionally, or physically. The impulse to push back as well as the impulse to retreat are very much rooted in your lower brain stem as a way of survival. It is a very human response. It is however, your most primitive response. It is a reaction often disconnected from the person you really are, the evolved person you want to be, the person you want to be when relating to others. And you know that, as primitive as your striking back or shutting down might be, or as the other person's assault or abandonment was, you both have other choices.

It just takes one of you to make a different choice, even after the fracture has occurred. Perhaps even especially after the injury has occurred. It only takes one, perhaps you, strong enough to invite dialogue. Through quality dialogue—being engaged, centered, grounded and clear—you have the best chance at reconnecting to your best self, and the other person has the best chance of reconnecting to their best self. Together you both can attend to the fractures in your interaction. Whether the other emerges from their self-absorption, *you* can emerge from your self-absorption, recognize the other's situation, and possibly both of you will see the other as more human. It only takes one person to initiate the dialogue.

So, if there is a chance for dialogue with the other person, you might want to take it. If the other person offers you an opportunity to dialogue, you might want to take it. Maybe, maybe not. The timing might not be right for you. Your injury might need more time for healing. You might have other demands on your time that are more pressing. Sometimes it is just not possible—the person who injured you is someone you probably will never see again. But if you have the opportunity and you can make the space in your life for dialogue with one who injured you, being relational means that you take that opportunity—even in dealing with a bully as we discussed above, but also *especially* in situations where you are in a position of greater power in relation to the other. It can be a momentary exchange, taking seconds when the inconvenience was not a deep injury.

If you have the opportunity and you can make the space in your life for dialogue with one who injured you, being relational means that you take that opportunity—even in dealing with a bully.

Let's go back to your experience of being hurt by someone else. All relationships experience these moments—especially those relationships that are long term. So what happens in that moment? There is a natural cycle of personal conflict transformation that is familiar to you. You have experienced this many times. After the injury event, whether you fought back or shut down, you then retreat. It is a primitive instinct as part of our survival. You take a break from the person, you retreat to the cave to lick your wounds. This can be momentary or this retreat can be hours, or weeks, or years.

How long you disconnect from the other often depends on the messages being given to you by those that you surround yourself with. The messages may be dismissive: "Kiss and make up," or "It's not that bad," or "Move on, it's not worth it." The messages may feed your resentment: "Get your revenge—an eye for an eye," or "I told you so," or "How could you let them do that to you?" or "What did you expect?" The messages may be supportive and relational: "Sounds like you are really hurt by them; I wonder what they are thinking?" or "That's rough, is there anything I can do to help?" You choose to surround yourself with others who are supportive. Supportive of what? Supportive of your well-being and the well-being of the other person.

In the natural cycle of conflict transformation, you take the time to look hard at deeper vulnerabilities. You determine the meaning of your vulnerabilities and how they informed your interaction. Being forced by others to do or say anything prematurely robs you of this discernment. Your regained sense of personal strength naturally emerges, however, when you take or are given the chance to have a new meaningful interaction with the person who harmed you. Through relational dialogue, facilitated or on your own, you become strong again, the grip of the suffering lessens, you are able to soften the urge to strike back, the clutch that wants to attack. You experience the beginnings of forgiveness. Forgiveness of yourself and of the other person. It is often difficult, but always kind to both you and the other person. You release without bypassing. Your forgiving does not mean you forget. But you are no longer attached to the injury.

Being kind means forgiving injuries, but it is not always clear how to do it. It is highly personal and depends a great deal on the nature of the injury. Is it a minor inconvenience? Even if minor, does it touch an old nerve of a prior unhealed injury involving someone else? Has it happened enough times to now be serious? Or is it a serious injury with lasting consequences? Forgiveness has several elements and, like other aspects of being relational, it is helpful to get clear about what it is *not*.

Being forgiving does not mean you are lenient and tolerate injury just to avoid conflict with others. You aren't a doormat. You don't make the injury smaller than it is. You do not engage in bypasses such as "I'm fine" when you are not. You also don't make the injury larger than it is. But injuries have consequences, and you hope, and maybe insist, that someone who injures you takes responsibility for their actions. You don't *condone* bad behavior or abuse. You aren't an *enabler* to someone in their behavior that is harmful to you or to themselves in ways that affect you. You are grounded, so you take your concerns directly to the other person and you engage with them in dialogue if possible. But you don't just say, "It's okay; I'll get over it," while allowing someone to continue hurting you without consequences. Your *tolerance* has limits, even as your *kindness* does not. Being forgiving, while it obviously does not mean that you impose retributive punishment and correction, it also does not mean that you just let things slide. If you have the power to impose a consequence, you do so with kindness.

Being forgiving does not mean you are lenient and tolerate injury just to avoid conflict with others. You aren't a doormat.

Finding the balance between compassion and healthy boundaries can be hard, especially with people you care about. Ask any parent. Recall our discussion earlier about being grounded and having healthy boundaries. You have options and you get clear about them. Being kind means that, in making a decision about how to deal with the person who injured you, you ask a few questions:

- "Is my response going to injure *them*?" (If yes, then you keep thinking about *better* ways to use your power to promote healing.)
- "Is my response likely to influence them not to injure *me* again?" (Hopefully the answer is yes, if not, then look harder and keep thinking more creatively about your response.)
- "Is my response likely to influence them not to injure *someone else*?" (Hopefully you answer yes because being relational means you are concerned not only about yourself, but also others who may be affected by your decisions. If not then, again, keep thinking more creatively about your response.)

You have power and you use it creatively. You use your power to promote your own healing in body, mind, and spirit. You use it to connect with the other in a way that allows them to see you as a person who has been wounded. You use it to help you see the other as a person—a person who might have a story that helps you understand their actions. You use your power to influence the other not to harm you or others like you again. That is kindness and a relational use of power. The outcome might not be as you wish—the person may not show any remorse, they may not say they're sorry, they might not change as quickly as you want—but you will give a sincere *effort to foster healing and reconciliation.* That is positive transformation of conflict—it is the essence of victim-offender reconciliation and restorative justice[24], whether or not the injury is serious or the consequences are lasting. Being relational embraces the belief that people have capacity to change,

24 See *www.RestorativeJustice.org* and the work of Ron and Roxanne Claassen—*http://Peace.Fresno.edu* and *www.DisciplineThatRestores.org*.

whether in that interactional moment or later when you may or may not see it, hear it, or experience it.

> Being relational embraces the belief that people have capacity to change, whether in that interactional moment or later when you may or may not see it, hear it, or experience it.

You might be saying, "That sounds nice, but how do I actually influence someone not to harm me or another again?" You can do it in many ways—especially when you are in a position of greater power—as you often are as a winner. The injury represents *a break in the trust relationship* between you and the other. There was something you *expected* from the other, you did not get it, and you were harmed. Your goal is to *reestablish that trust.* You have a desire to trust them again, and being kind means you take an active role in helping them provide a new basis for your trust and trust from others. So think about how you could trust them again. *How can they earn your trust back?* How can you be strong enough to be vulnerable enough to help them earn that trust?

Being relational means you help others build trust by *building their capacity to care for and desire not to harm* others. In some situations, the other might be you. This capacity is *not based on fear of punishment.* Forget about ***doing justice.*** Imposing harsh punishment and motivating the other to stay in line based on coercive fear is the easy way out. While it can be effective, it is often only short term. You choose instead to take the more difficult path of engagement with the other, *educating* them about how to build trust, *showing* them you care about bringing

> You help others build trust by *building their capacity to care for and desire not to harm* others.

them back into your trust and your community. You might have to do that from a safe distance through correspondence or face-to-face dialogue facilitated by a mediator. You don't leave yourself in a harmful relationship. You create healthy boundaries. You can make *incremental agreements to rebuild* confidence—small steps to reestablish trust. You praise success and, when there are failures, you take a step back and ask them to work harder.

The other might not come along with you on this journey to rebuild trust, but you offer it. You *persist* in offering it. They make their choice. It might take a long time. They may have many barriers to overcome—anger (at you or themselves), shame, fear, mistrust, insecurity, physical or mental illness, past wounds (physical, mental and spiritual), excess testosterone, and even cultural norms favoring aggression. Being relational means you believe that, for lasting positive change to occur, wrongdoing is healed only with a loving response. So you stick with it.

Being relational means you believe that, for lasting positive change to occur, wrongdoing is healed only with a loving response.

Along the way in this journey, as a conscious choice, *you release yourself and the other from the ongoing effect of the injury.* You release your need to hold on to the experience of the injury. You don't let an injury define you as a person. You don't let an injury define your group. Being a victim is not your identity and, while you don't deny your suffering, you don't choose it. You allow it, but then you let go of it. It is like the grieving process. Maybe you go through all the stages: denial, anger—at the other and yourself—bargaining, and depression. Maybe you cycle through them more than once. Maybe not, depending on the nature and severity of your injury. You talk to people who care for you, knowing that a path to your healing is through their empathy and connection with you. Your injury is not a secret you hold privately, even if you think that you are partly responsible for it. You are humble and know there is no shame in sharing your hurts or your failures. And *you get there somehow*, knowing that your release of the injury is *essential* to your healing and happiness.

With that release you can begin to treat the other as a trusted brother or sister again. You are also open and trusting as you go forward and encounter others whom you might view with mistrust because of the injury you suffered. You *live without prejudice* toward others who, in your mind, are like the one that hurt you. You reject labels. You are centered and grounded. You don't triangle and generalize your injury by applying it to a group.

If you struggle with this process of releasing your feelings of resentment, you can *think about how you do it with people close to you*. In a similar way as we discussed earlier with being generous, use your imagination. For us, the easiest example is our children. How does it feel when we forgive them? How does it feel when they forgive us? It is gentle, connected, with a smile that says, "It's okay, I still love you," knowing their internal well of goodness is deep and our internal well of goodness is deep. Forgiving or being forgiven by someone you are not as close to may not be exactly like that, but you can start there to move toward seeing the other as someone who can forgive you, someone you can forgive. Hold onto that thought, build on it. Find a place for peace within you. Allow for the quality of being open to emerge, a change in your experience with the other that makes room for the possibility of a better future interaction.

Being Kind Is Being Gentle

Forgiving is a gentle way of dealing with injury and being kind means you are gentle in all the ways you deal with others. As we talked about earlier, you are strong and brave and you don't use your power to harm others. In being clear, you are honest—in a gentle way. You are not brutally honest. You are also not soft or a push-over. You don't crumble and cave in. You find a *middle way of being*, between the extremes, that is good for both you and others. That way is gentle. The Seven Ways of Being Relational are your how-to for that middle way. They create a bridge, an opening, to something new in the interaction that did not exist before.

For winners like you, lasting positive change in your family, workplace, community and world starts with you—being gentle in how you use your power because what you do affects others. You want that effect to be positive. You want to maximize well-being for both self and other. Competition that crushes and oppresses others is not positive. There is a time and a place for competing—in sports, in games, in business, in sales, in donations, in votes—but even in these arenas there are limits. Using your power to get all that you can for yourself out of an interaction with another might seem good in the ***short*** run, but in the ***long*** run it leaves them poor and bitter and you rich and hollow. So you choose to be gentle in your dealings with others—embodying everything that is positively transformative—being generous, humble and kind.

It goes back to where we started, being relational versus being transactional.

You consider your interactions, all of them. You are aware of your power currencies and the many temptations to maximize your own self-interest over another or at the expense of another. You are discerning and you consider how it feels for you when others maximize their self-interests over yours. You know that maximizing self-interest in the short run might get you what you think you want. Maybe not.

Being relational, you consider yourself and the impact on the other. You believe you can get what you want without disadvantaging others. You are thoughtful and discerning. You put effort into quality engagement. You have the ability to both look back and to imagine forward, and you have the capacity of self-observation in the moment. You practice being relational in every interaction. When you do, you enter into a sense of connectedness with others. A sense of *ease*. Being relational brings ease to interactions. Others feel it too. You maximize well-being. You are inspired and you inspire others to become more open. You create openness. With openness comes potential. You anticipate that something good will happen when you engage relationally. It is unknown exactly what that is or will be. You are okay with that. You know you can positively expect the unexpected.

Be relational. You know how to do it. We hope we helped you with that.

It's a very good way to be—for you, for others, for everyone.

Questions for Your Consideration

In exploring Being Kind, consider the following questions. If you are not sure about your answers, go back and visit the chapter.

- What are your main sources of power in relation to others? How do you use them?
- What uses of power do you consider "out of bounds?" Why?
- How do you respond to a bully?
- What sources of power do you call upon when dealing with a bully?
- What is the consequence of forcing people to do things that they don't want to do?
- Is it good to "Speak softly and carry a big stick?" Why? Why not?
- How do you use your power in relation to people over whom you have power and in relation to people you perceive as having less or equal power in relation to you?
- What is your response when you encounter people who need help?
- Do you agree with the statement "There is evil in the world that can only be dealt with through force, and violence if necessary." Why? Why not?
- How does compassion require courage?
- How do you deal with time demands in deciding how to deal with other people?
- How do you respond to an injury or inconvenience caused by another person?
- How can you help people who injure you to earn back your trust?

Epilogue

If you come to this page after reading the entire book, you probably have an idea of where we are coming from, what beliefs underlie our concepts of being relational. If you skipped from the beginning of the book to the end, you might have a clue, but maybe aren't quite sure. For us, all that is "being relational" comes from the example and teaching of Jesus Christ. You don't have to believe in Jesus Christ to be relational since *Being Relational* is premised on a belief in the potential for unity across all lines of belief and culture in the struggle to live in a way that seeks quality interaction and lasting change, maximizing well-being for both yourself and others.

We believe that Jesus walked the Earth as a man some 2000 years ago, but that he also was indeed who he claimed to be—the Son of God. So he is a singular figure in human history, unlike any other. Jesus forces a choice upon us. Either we say he is who he says that he is—God's son—or we say he is a dangerous and delusional man.

We made our choice and we respect yours whether or not you agree. You don't need to agree in order to be relational.

No matter what one might say about his divinity, we would say that Jesus embodied being relational in his life, in the way he related to others and in the way he gave himself up for death by crucifixion with forgiveness. He was in all ways engaged, centered, grounded, clear, generous, humble, and kind. He never used his power to enrich himself or cause harm to others through violence or otherwise. He never used his power to coerce anyone to do anything they would not choose to do on their own. He influenced others with his acts of mercy and kindness, both commonplace and miraculous. He suffered death while asking God to forgive those who crucified him. He gave of himself completely to others.

Jesus also taught us to be relational with his words. He gave us one commandment—**Love one another**. That's what it's all about—even our enemies and those who hurt and threaten us—the bullies. He taught us to turn the other cheek. He taught us that we are all one body and that we are our brother's keeper. He taught us that evil will always pass and we will never be alone. We might not live up to his example, but we can try. We will try and hope you will too. Peace be with you.

Sending love,
Louise and Bill

P.S. We have one more thing we would like to share with you . . .

ORANS—The Image of Being Relational

As you might guess, writing this book has been an exciting journey for us. It has been many years in the making. When talking to our friends and colleagues from many walks of life, we often get a question like, "Is there a simple way to explain what it means to be relational?" We have struggled with this because, as you know from reading the book, being relational involves a wide range of values, attitudes, and practices. It cannot be reduced to one quick phrase. Nonetheless, we wanted to discover some way immediately to communicate the concept.

ORANS came to us. The word refers to a posture of openness and vulnerability, strength and grace. It is commonly associated with communities participating together in prayer. Here we are together in this pose:

Throughout the book and on the cover, you may have noticed ORANS and the image we have developed with the help of some wonderful designers, Amber Shriver and husband Nathan, creative director at Under Armour, to abstractly represent ORANS. We think it captures the essence of being relational.

ORANS

We hope that the ORANS image, wherever it appears, inspires and reminds us to Be Relational.

We hope that the ORANS image, if you choose to wear it or display it in some way, will let others know that you believe that being relational is a good way to be and that you hope that they will be relational in dealing with you.

It is a symbol of solidarity and unity across all lines of belief and culture in the struggle to live in a way that seeks quality interaction and lasting change, maximizing well-being for both yourself and others. Check it out at *www.JoinORANS.org*.

Suggested Reading/ References

Angelica, Mother M. and Christine Allison. *Mother Angelica's Answers, Not Promises.* New York: Harper and Row, 1987.

Bowen, Will. *A Complaint Free World: How to Stop Complaining and Start Enjoying the Life You Always Wanted.* New York: Doubleday, 2007.

Bush, Robert A. and Joseph Folger. *The Promise of Mediation: Responding to Conflict Through Empowerment and Recognition.* San Francisco: Jossey-Bass, 1994.

Bush, Robert A. and Joseph Folger. *The Promise of Mediation: The Transformative Approach to Conflict.* San Francisco: Jossey-Bass, 2005.

Cain, Susan. *Quiet: The Power of Introverts in a World that Can't Stop Talking.* New York: Crown, 2012.

Collins, Jim. *Good to Great: Why Some Companies Make the Leap—and Others Don't.* New York: Harper Business, 2001.

Covey, Stephen. *The Seven Habits of Highly Effective People: Restoring the Character Ethic.* New York: Simon and Schuster, 1989.

Craver, Charles B. *Effective Legal Negotiation and Settlement.* Newark, NJ: LexisNexis, 2005.

Crum, Thomas F. *The Magic of Conflict: Turning a Life of Work into a Work of Art.* New York: Simon and Schuster, 1987.

Das, Lama S. *Awakening the Buddha Within: Tibetan Wisdom for the Western World.* New York: Broadway Books, 1997.

Evans, Alice F., Robert Evans, and Ronald Kraybill. *Peace Skills: Leaders Guide.* San Francisco: Jossey-Bass, 2001.

Faber, Adele and Elaine Mazlish. *Siblings Without Rivalry: How to Help Your Children Live Together so You Can Live Too.* New York: W.W. Norton & Co., 1987.

Fisher, Roger, William Ury, and Bruce Patton. *Getting to Yes: Negotiating Agreement Without Giving In.* New York: Penguin Books, 1991.

Fox, Erica Ariel. *Winning from Within: A Breakthrough Method for Leading, Living, and Lasting Change.* New York: Harper Business, 2013.

Gandhi, Mahatma and Louis Fischer. *The Essential Gandhi: An Anthology of His Writings on His Life, Work, and Ideas.* New York: Vintage Books, 1983.

Gladwell, Malcolm. *Blink: The Power of Thinking Without Thinking.* New York: Little, Brown and Co., 2005.

Goleman, Daniel. *Emotional Intelligence.* New York: Bantam Books, 1995.

Haidt, Jonathan. *The Righteous Mind: Why Good People are Divided by Politics and Religion.* New York: Pantheon Books, 2012.

Katie, Byron and Stephen Mitchell. *Loving What Is: Four Questions That Can Change Your Life.* New York: Three Rivers Press, 2002.

Lederach, John Paul. *The Little Book of Conflict Transformation.* Intercourse, PA: Good Books, 2003.

Mehta, Pavithra and Suchrita Shenoy. *Infinite Vision: How Aravind Became the World's Greatest Business Case for Compassion.* San Francisco: Berrett-Koehler, 2011.

Menkel-Meadow, Carrie and Michael Wheeler. *What's Fair: Ethics for Negotiators.* San Francisco: Jossey-Bass, 2004.

Nagle-Lechman, Barbara A. *Conflict and Resolution.* New York: Aspen Law and Business, 1997.

Palmer, Helen. *The Enneagram: Understanding Yourself and the Others in Your Life.* San Francisco: HarperCollins, 1991.

Pirsig, Robert M. *Zen and the Art of Motorcycle Maintenance: An Inquiry into Values.* New York: HarperCollins, 1974.

Ruiz, Don Miguel. *The Four Agreements: A Practical Guide to Personal Freedom.* San Rafael, CA: Amber-Allen Pub., 1997.

Shadyac, Tom. *Life's Operating Manual: With the Fear and Truth Dialogues.* Australia: Hay House Inc., 2013.

Siegel, Daniel J. *The Developing Mind: How Relationships and the Brain Interact to Shape Who We Are.* New York: Guilford Press, 1999.

Siegel, Daniel J. *Mindsight: The New Science of Personal Transformation.* New York: Bantam Books, 2010.

Siegel, Daniel J. *Pocket Guide to Interpersonal Neurobiology: An Integrative Handbook of the Mind.* New York: W.W. Norton & Co., 2012.

Sinek, Simon. *Start with Why: How Great Leaders Inspire Everyone to Take Action.* New York: Portfolio, 2009.

Tolle, Eckhart. *Practicing the Power of Now: Essential Teachings, Meditations, and Exercises from the Power of Now.* Novato, CA: New World Library, 2001.

Whitmire, Catherine. *Practicing Peace: A Devotional Walk Through the Quaker Tradition.* Notre Dame, IN: Sorin Books, 2007.

Wilmot, William and Joyce Hocker (n.d.). *Interpersonal Conflict.* 7th ed. New York: McGraw-Hill, 2005.

Index

J

K

L

M

N

O

Printed in Great Britain
by Amazon

43129664R00149